NOT YOUR NORMAL FAMILY

A single Asperger woman's adoption of two Down's boys

Fiona Barrington

Foreword by Jennifer Rees Larcombe

Visit us online at www.authorsonline.co.uk

An Authors OnLine Book

Copyright © Fiona Barrington 2008

Cover design by Hayes Design ©

All rights reserved. No part of this publication may be reproduced, stored in a retrieval system, or transmitted in any form or by any means, electronic, mechanical, photocopy, recording or otherwise, without prior written permission of the copyright owner. Nor can it be circulated in any form of binding or cover other than that in which it is published and without similar condition including this condition being imposed on a subsequent purchaser.

The moral rights of the authors have been asserted.

Scripture quotations taken from the
HOLY BIBLE, NEW INTERNATIONAL VERSION.
Copyright © 1973, 1978, 1984 by International Bible Society.
Used by permission of Hodder & Stoughton Publishers,
A member of the Hachette Livre UK Group.
All rights reserved.
"NIV" is a registered trademark of International Bible Society.
UK trademark number 1448790.

ISBN 978-07552-0421-2

Authors OnLine Ltd
19 The Cinques
Gamlingay, Sandy
Bedfordshire SG19 3NU
England

This book is also available in e-book format, details of which are available at www.authorsonline.co.uk

CONTENTS

Foreword v
Author's Note vii
Chapter 1 1
   Early Memories
Chapter 2 8
   The Winter of 1962/63
Chapter 3 18
   Engulfed by Fear
Chapter 4 25
   Escape into Fantasy
Chapter 5 30
   Help at Last
Chapter 6 36
   A New Life
Chapter 7 42
   A New Interest
Chapter 8 47
   The Cedars
Chapter 9 52
   The Long Wait for Mr Right
Chapter 10 62
   A New Hope
Chapter 11 68
   The Search Begins
Chapter 12 73
   "I don't like Thursdays"
Chapter 13 78
   "Don't Give Up!"
Chapter 14 85
   Daniel
Chapter 15 91
   "Mummy"
Chapter 16 96
   Second Time Around

Chapter 17 101
   Matthew
Chapter 18 106
   Pride Comes Before a Fall
Chapter 19 113
   Back to Work
Chapter 20 118
   Delights and Difficulties
Chapter 21 125
   Another Disability
Chapter 22 132
   Life Goes On
Chapter 23 139
   "Do you have Asperger Syndrome?"
Chapter 24 144
   Coming Out
Chapter 25 151
   Looking to the Future
Appendix 1 - What is Asperger Syndrome? 159
Appendix 2   Useful Organisations 167

Foreword

It was their laughter and joy in tiny things - like butterflies and a little red ladybird that made me realise they were 'Not your normal family'. We were on holiday with Fiona and her two Down's Syndrome sons. They were little more than babies and, as a single mum, she certainly had her hands full, but it was their sheer uncomplicated enjoyment of life that made that holiday such a special memory for me.

I came home with a great admiration for Fiona and her decision to adopt those two adorable boys. Over the years my respect for her has grown and, if possible, it has increased still further through reading this book. Adopting two boys as a single parent would be a major challenge for anyone, but on top of that Fiona also had to handle her own Asperger Syndrome and the complex problems of living with Downs as well as her long fight with Adoption Red Tape. This is an amazing story written by an amazing lady!

I have two friends whose husbands have recently been diagnosed with Asperger Syndrome. While the diagnosis is grim it has actually been a great relief to them both. Up until now they saw their husbands as 'difficult' and constantly urged them to 'turn over a new leaf and try and love other people more – be more reasonable and less stubborn!' Realising that they had married someone with a recognizable condition that made various kinds of 'normal' human thinking and behaviour impossible they both relaxed and began to concentrate upon, and appreciate, their husbands' many good qualities instead of focusing on their problems. There will probably be many people who read this book who know, or are related to, someone with Asperger Syndrome and who are finding it extremely difficult to understand what makes them tick. I suspect that this book will be a major eye opener to you, as it certainly has been to me. I intended to skip through it quickly but found myself becoming so absorbed and involved in the life of this far from normal family that I was forced to savour every page

slowly and carefully. It is not only a worthwhile and thought provoking book but it also makes a thoroughly enjoyable read!
   Jennifer Rees Larcombe
   2008

Author's Note

This is my true story. Although my personal preference is for complete openness, I am aware of the need to protect the privacy of the people mentioned in the book. I have therefore changed all the names, including the name of the Care home where I once worked and am writing under a pseudonym. All other details including dates are unchanged. Those who know me personally will readily identify me, since my story is so unusual. Whilst I am happy with this, I would ask them to respect the privacy of my sons.

My hope is that this book will help people to understand and value those of us who differ from the norm and will encourage those who have been through similar experiences to mine.

If you wish to contact me, please email f.barrington@ntlworld.com. Those without internet access may contact me through Authors OnLine Ltd, 19 The Cinques, Gamlingay, Sandy, Beds SG19 3NU, England.

Chapter 1

Early Memories

My first day on this earth was very nearly my last.

When my mother went into labour early one Wednesday morning in the autumn of 1956, she first cycled to the shops to stock up with food and then returned home to wait for what should have been a repetition of my sister Rachel's trouble-free arrival three years earlier. After my six year old brother Simon's difficult breech birth, when she had been surrounded by gawping, mainly male, medical students, my mother had no wish for another hospital delivery, but by noon on the Thursday it was clear that something was wrong.

Soon after the ambulance took my mother to hospital my father, who was at work, was informed that either mother or baby would not survive. Subsequent failure to detect a heartbeat seemed to confirm this gloomy prophecy and a decision was taken to yank the baby out with forceps. Against all the odds we both survived and apart from scratches from the forceps I appeared unharmed.

My father, rushing back from the office, was naturally anxious to see his wife, after so nearly losing her, as well as meeting his new daughter, but he had a dilemma. He was a deacon of the local Baptist church and they had a meeting that night. Since his earliest days he had been taught that when duty and inclination clash, duty must always come first. As a result, believing that was where his duty lay, he went to the meeting, a decision my mother found hard to forgive.

Recently I read that a high proportion of children with Asperger's had difficult births and I wonder what damage may have resulted from the trauma of my arrival. Yet the descriptions I have heard of my paternal grandfather provide a bigger clue. As well as being a brilliant mathematician, he was a perfectionist with very poor social skills and a rigid

1

moral code. In character my grandfather closely resembled his own father and he married his first cousin on his father's side. Whilst my grandmother was a friendly, sociable person who was the complete opposite of her husband, the chance of any genetic peculiarities in the family being passed on to their descendants must have been increased by their marriage. From an early age I was told that I had inherited my grandfather's mathematical gifts and it now seems highly likely that my Asperger Syndrome was part of that inheritance. Whilst I am his only descendant with an official diagnosis, it is my opinion that most of his male descendants also share the Asperger traits in varying degrees.

My earliest memories are of Sunday school, to which I was sent from the age of two. There was one little American boy who puzzled me greatly, as nearly every week he would ask to go to the bathroom. I was not aware of any bath in the church building, unless you counted the pool beneath the floor of the church in which people were baptised, and why would anyone want a bath in the middle of Sunday school?

Another thing I noticed at Sunday school was the collection. Each week we put our pennies, thruppenny bits (coins worth three old pence) and sixpences into two baskets, then halfway through the meeting an elderly man would put his head round the door and take the baskets away. The teachers told me that the money was for God, so I reasoned that this man must be an angel who would take the money up to heaven. Looking back, I think he may have been the church secretary, who far from being angelic was a grumpy man who had once badly upset my father.

As well as being a deacon my father was the church organist (and he often took on other jobs in the church as well). Once in the middle of the service, the church secretary had called out to my father, telling him to play the next hymn more slowly. Although he appeared very confident in public and was sometimes accused of being insensitive due to his difficulties in reading body language, my father was actually hypersensitive to criticism and lived in dread of a similar attack. Despite the fact that I had probably met this man and been introduced to him as an ordinary mortal, the difficulty I have had all my life in recognising faces would have stopped me from connecting the angel with the grumpy church secretary.

By the age of three I was accustomed to walking to church and to my sister's school, since we had no car and my pushchair had been stolen on holiday. We had left it at the top of the cliff while we went down the steps to the beach, only to find it had vanished when we returned. My parents could ill afford a new pushchair so we had to manage without one. Although my sister's school was nearly a mile away, I coped well with the double journey, except on alternate Mondays, when the road sweeping machine came along our street. There was something about the whirring brushes that terrified me and I lived in dread of these days.

My parents also had to cope with my fear of dogs which started for no apparent reason when I was three years old. I have since discovered that this is a very common fear in children with Asperger Syndrome or other forms of autism. Our hypersensitivity to noise and touch can make a barking, leaping dog impossible to endure, even without the additional fear of being bitten.

Another source of terror at this time was any journey by train. Whilst not fearing the vehicle itself, I became hysterical at the thought that it might suddenly start moving while we were getting on and carry me away, leaving my parents on the platform, or vice versa. Years later, my mother commented on my early fear, expressing sadness that I had trusted them so little as to fear that they would abandon me. I looked at her in astonishment.

"Of course I trusted you. It was the train I didn't trust, fearing that it would start moving and separate us before we could all get on."

She then explained that the guard always checked that all the doors were closed before allowing the train to start. If only I had known that at the time but of course my parents did not understand the reason for my fear.

Soon after my fourth birthday, my mother enrolled me at the local nursery school. The Principal informed her that there were few places available and she had to give priority to children in greatest need, either due to their home situation or the child's own problems. My mother confessed that she could give no reason why I needed nursery school, other than the fact that I was bored at home, yet we were offered a place, the Principal saying: "We do need some normal children." Little did she know!

If my mother was hoping for some time to herself whilst I was at nursery school, she was soon disappointed, as within a month I had caught German measles (rubella) which I generously shared with my brother and sister. Within days of Simon and Rachel returning to school I was home again, this time with measles. Missing nursery school didn't bother me at all. Despite enjoying some of the activities there were two major drawbacks: the lunches and the toilets.

All three of us children were fussy eaters, my brother and I being the most reluctant to try out new things. At home my mother would never force us to eat things we disliked and would usually provide some alternative. Sometimes she felt that she should be stricter and let us go hungry, but we were all so thin that she didn't dare risk our health. Although she was criticised for spoiling us at the time, looking back I realize that she instinctively did the right thing. Refusal of various foods by children with Asperger's is usually due to heightened sensitivity to certain tastes and textures as well as fear of the unknown, rather than a behaviour problem. At the nursery school, not only were we expected to eat whatever we were given, but also those who failed to finish the first course were denied any pudding. To make matters worse, the nicest puddings always seemed to be served on days when the first course was inedible. Sheer hunger compelled me to try a few things I would never touch at home, but some tastes and textures revolted me so much that I would rather starve than sample them, so sometimes I would have no lunch at all.

The toilets were another source of anxiety. There was no toilet paper in the cubicles and children had to ask a member of staff if they needed any. We were also told that it would only be given when we had done what was euphemistically called "jobs". (A different euphemism was used at home.) Once I had the temerity to ask for toilet paper when I had not fulfilled the necessary requirement and received a sharp scolding. Distressed and confused, I confided in my mother, who came up with a solution. She made some special pockets in some of my knickers so that I could take my own toilet paper to nursery school and not have to risk angering the staff again.

Although I made one friend at nursery school, a little girl a year younger than myself, generally I did not mix well with the others and often found myself alone. I also remember one of the staff telling me crossly that there were twenty five children in the school, not just one. It was a relief when the summer holidays began and I said goodbye to nursery school forever.

One good thing about the nursery school was that it made "big school" more attractive by comparison. The days were much more structured and I enjoyed the reading and sums, although the latter were always too easy. When we first arrived each of us was asked to show how far we could count and I was most annoyed to be stopped shortly after reaching one hundred when I could have gone on for much longer. The frustration of being held back and not allowed to progress at my own pace in maths continued throughout primary school. Fortunately my brother, Simon, shared my love of maths and would sometimes give me a lesson. Over the years I also learned a lot simply by studying numbers and noting their patterns.

Numbers held an endless fascination for me. There was the way that you could tell whether a number was a multiple of three simply by adding the digits. If the result was a multiple of three then so was the original number. Square numbers were particularly interesting. Long before I was able to prove it using algebra I learnt by observation that for any number N, if you multiply N+1 by N-1 the result is always N squared minus 1. As a small child, I used to amuse myself in church by counting the number of hats worn by the ladies. Later on, as my knowledge of maths grew, I started factorising the hymn numbers and working out which of them were primes.

The problem of school dinners continued during infant school. The children were not allowed to bring packed lunches and my mother said that I would have to wait until I was nearly eight and at junior school before she would allow me to walk back on my own and have lunch at home. At least there was no rule stopping you from having pudding if you hadn't eaten the first course, but on one occasion I was literally force fed with a spoonful of rice pudding by an exasperated dinner lady. Of all dishes, rice pudding was the one I loathed most, more for its looks and texture (which reminded me of vomit) than for its taste. My father had rice pudding poured over him on more than one occasion as part of a school performance, giving him a lifelong revulsion which has been shared by all his children.

Mercifully the force feeding episode was not repeated, but day after day I was made to sit at the table long after the others had gone out to play and endure the reproaches of the staff. Much as I dreaded adult disapproval, there were some foods I simply could not bear to eat and I would frequently arrive home nearly fainting with hunger.

Finding friends was no easier than it had been at nursery school. Whenever I asked a group of children if I could join them, I would get the reply "N O spells no."

I would immediately retort: "I know it does", annoyed by their attempts to be funny instead of giving a straightforward answer. Still, even this hurtful reply was preferable to the tactic used by some children in later years of simply ignoring me completely when I tried to talk to them. There was, however, one girl, Pam, who would sometimes play with me and between us we invented the cave game. In this game we were brothers who explored caves and kept finding hidden treasure. It was Pam's idea that we should be boys as she felt that exploring caves was a male pursuit. Whilst I enjoyed my friendship with Pam, I was often infuriated by her tall stories, one of which was that she was really the daughter of John Lennon. I knew this was impossible and didn't hesitate to tell her so, but she kept on with the story.

In the classroom, one of the activities we enjoyed was playing with the toy shop. On a couple of occasions Pam showed me a cardboard sixpence which she had taken from the till. Inspired by her example and wanting to impress her, I stole a cardboard half-crown. To my disappointment Pam didn't seem at all pleased. Soon afterwards I was filled with remorse and wanted to put the cardboard coin back, but by then I had chewed it so much that this was no longer an option.

Pam's mother disapproved of the friendship, largely because of my behaviour at Pam's sixth birthday party. I have always found group situations difficult, much preferring one-to-one and I arrived at the party tired out after a day in London watching the Lord Mayor's show from my father's office. I don't recall doing anything outrageous at the party, but was so irritable and bad tempered that everyone greeted my mother's return to collect me with an audible sigh of relief. When Pam's mother offered me a handkerchief as a parting gift, my usual preference for truth over tact led to the response: "I don't want that."

As a result, Pam's mother decided I was not a fit companion for her precious daughter although there was nothing she could do to stop us mixing at school.

A few weeks after this disastrous party, just after Christmas 1962, snow arrived with a vengeance heralding the start of the most traumatic year of my early childhood.

Chapter 2

The Winter of 1962/63

Initially we children were delighted with the snow, but the novelty soon wore off as the weeks turned into months and we still had to get up in a freezing cold, unheated bedroom and trudge through a mile of snow each day to reach school. Great lumps of ice appeared in the school milk and then the water in the pipes of the outside toilets froze and some men were sent to fix them. Going into the toilets at lunch time I was horrified to find men in there, opening the doors (which had no locks). The fear of one of the men bursting in made it impossible for me to go to the toilet and I had to endure afternoon school in great discomfort.

Throughout this period the school remained open, even though closing it would have caused relatively little inconvenience since most mothers in those days did not work outside the home. By contrast, during my sons' schooldays, the slightest snowfall would lead to a telephone call at work telling me to come home immediately because they were closing the school. With the snow lying for three months in 1963, it would clearly have been impractical to close the school for that length of time, but surely they should not have expected us to go to school when the toilets were out of action?

There were many other sources of stress within the family. As well as facing the double journey to school and back in the snow each day, my mother had to deal with the cat, who couldn't go outside to relieve herself because the snow was too deep and often made messes in the house instead of using the litter tray. In the end the strain became too much and my mother asked the vet to put the cat down. My father was unable to play the organ, since burst pipes in the church meant we had to meet in the church hall for several months while repairs were carried out. Music was one of the great loves of his life and he felt the deprivation keenly, as well as fretting constantly that the organ would be permanently damaged by being exposed to a damp atmosphere for so long. Finally, as my brother hit puberty, all the tensions in relationships between the family members suddenly escalated.

The problems had all started with my sister's birth. Three year old Simon was sent away to his grandmother's house for a few days and returned to find his place usurped by a small baby. Naturally, he responded with jealousy and attacked the intruder at every opportunity. What made things worse was that despite being highly intelligent (he later obtained a BSc, 2 MSc's and an MPhil in maths and related subjects), at the age of three he had very little speech. My mother has always attributed this to the fact that he had no companion but her in his early years and she was too lonely and depressed to talk to him very much. Whatever the reason, the lack of speech meant that he could only express his feelings through actions and these actions were badly misunderstood.

If my parents had experienced different childhoods or had close friends who were also parents, they might have realised that my brother's actions were normal and understandable, but neither of them had received a typical upbringing. My father had been an only child for fourteen years and when his younger brother finally arrived, he felt more like an uncle than a brother and doted on the baby. Furthermore, his own father's harshness towards him and inability to tolerate any childish whims and weaknesses made it hard for him to deal gently with his son, particularly when that son was attacking his beloved baby daughter.

My mother's parents had been missionaries in India and she and her older brother and sister started boarding school at the age of seven. For their secondary education they were sent back to England and after their parents returned to India they spent their holidays with separate guardians. My mother was more fortunate than her older siblings as the outbreak of war in September 1939, on the day of her arrival in England, meant that her parents were unable to return to India for some time. She still attended a boarding school but at least saw her parents in the holidays. Even when my grandfather went back to India in 1942, his wife was not allowed to go with him as it was too dangerous. The subsequent sinking of one of the ships in his convoy by a U-boat showed that these concerns were justified. Two years later, when my mother was sixteen, my grandmother was finally able to join her husband in India and my mother was left with her guardians, who were my father's parents. Although my father had by then left home and joined the navy, they met often enough to fall in love. Having spent so little of her childhood with her parents and siblings, my mother had an idealised view of family life and it was a tremendous shock when her "perfect" family of a boy and a girl fell so far short of her dream.

My parents' reaction to Simon's jealousy was to punish him, which of course made it much worse and he changed into a deeply unhappy and angry child. My arrival on the scene three years later improved matters a little, as Simon and Rachel welcomed me at first, although Simon soon realised that both my parents had a preference for girls, however hard they tried not to show it. We had some good times together, when Simon would tell us stories or teach me some maths, but it took very little to arouse his anger and I lived in fear of his scornful tongue and violent temper. My own inability to read body language means that I cannot tell when I am making someone angry, until they start shouting, hitting me or saying something nasty. This made my brother's anger quite unpredictable, leading to great insecurity. With the onset of puberty, the surge of testosterone made it even more difficult for him to control his temper and family rows increased.

In one way my sister and I were the lucky ones as we knew that whatever we did to provoke Simon, if he hit us he would always get the blame. In my case the provocation was usually (although not always) unintentional, but Simon may not have realised this. My parents again overreacted, my mother predicting that he would end up murdering someone, which is probably why even as an adult I had several nightmares in which he would try to kill me. In fact, he has probably gained better control over his temper in adulthood than I have, largely as a result of his Christian faith and a willingness to forgive our parents for their mistakes.

It was after the snow had finally gone and the summer term was drawing to an end that matters came to a head. One day a supply teacher arrived as our usual teacher was ill. For some reason she told us at one point that we were not to touch our pencils. The problem was that I had just received some work back and the regular teacher insisted that the moment our work was returned we should start on the corrections. Whatever I did I would have to disobey one of them, so I decided it was more important to obey the regular teacher and picked up the pencil. Immediately I was spotted and called to the front of the class.

Along with two or three others who had also aroused her anger, I was ordered to tell her my name so that she could write it down. My surname is a very unusual one and at the best of times I need to repeat it and spell it out for people. Even then, they invariably mishear some of the letters and spell it wrong. Being already nervous, it was only after several attempts to tell her my name that she was finally able to write it down and by that time she was furious with me, telling me I was the worst behaved of the lot. In great distress I went home and flatly refused to go back to school until that teacher had left.

For a week after the incident with the supply teacher I remained at home. Then one evening my mother returned from a parents' evening with the news that my regular teacher had returned and told her I had come top in the end of year tests. After that, I agreed to return to school for the last few days of term, but for months I remained in a highly nervous state, clinging to my mother and needing to visit the toilet with alarming frequency.

Other people could not fail to notice my frequent trips to the toilet and Simon teased me unmercifully, calling the toilet my home and asking if he should pay me rent each time he went there. I can still recall the disgust and anger in his voice when he caught me committing the unspeakable crime of visiting the toilet twice within one hour. Teachers also became impatient over my frequent requests to be excused and I was soon convinced that this problem was abnormal and shameful, something that would make people despise me, or even worse, laugh at me.

After several months my nerves improved and the trips to the toilet became less frequent, although the anxiety whenever I was far from a toilet remained, making any outings stressful. My brother's teasing continued, but there were also times when our common interests drew us together.

As well as our love of maths, Simon and I now shared an interest in pop music and I loved listening to his records, although there was one whose title puzzled me: *The best of the Beach Boys*. The record cover showed a picture of five men and I thought "If these five men are the best Beach Boys, it must be a very big group." Yet when I asked Simon how many were in the group altogether he said "Five", which baffled me even more. It was only when looking back years later it finally dawned on me that although the title said *The best of the Beach Boys*, what it meant was *The best of the Beach Boys' songs*. As has happened so often in my life, my literal mind had been unable to move from what was actually said or written to grasp what was meant. Life would be so much simpler if everyone said exactly what they meant, which would be the case if people with Asperger's were in the majority.

My sister Rachel had been my main companion in my early years. Although we had plenty of quarrels we spent a lot of time playing together with our dolls and talking in our room after we had been sent to bed. We enjoyed many outings together to the park or the shops, my parents trusting her to look after me. Now, however, she was beginning to grow away from me, preferring books to dolls and starting to want her own bedroom. My increasing jealousy was also driving a wedge between us, as I sensed that my parents found her easier to love. She made friends more easily than I did and sometimes friends I brought home would end up playing with her. When I was about nine, by mutual agreement I moved out of our bedroom and slept downstairs in the playroom.

One bone of contention at this time was my parents' insistence that I cleaned my own shoes from the age of nine. Whilst I had no particular objection to this task, I was convinced that my sister had only been compelled to clean her shoes from the age of ten (although she claimed it was from age eight) and my sense of justice was outraged. When my parents proved implacable, I suggested a compromise: if they agreed not to force me to clean my shoes until I was ten, I would do it on a voluntary basis from age nine. Sadly they did not agree.

By now I had also abandoned dolls in favour of books, particularly those written by Enid Blyton. Whilst I found reading easy, some of the expressions used in the books confused me. If someone was said to be hitting the nail on the head, I would assume they were actually wielding a hammer and striking a nail with it. As well as loving Enid Blyton's school stories I devoured the adventure books, including the *Famous Five* series, even though I worked out that George and the other children should have been well into their twenties by the time they had their last adventure. (Of course, in real life I would have been terrified of a lively, noisy dog like Timmy and would have clashed badly with George, who in addition to her more obvious gender identity problem had almost certainly inherited her father's Asperger Syndrome.) As I became increasingly solitary both at home and at school I began to invent fantasy worlds inspired by the books I read, in which I had all the friends I needed, or an identical twin sister who understood and accepted me completely.

Around this time the family next door moved away. Both Rachel and I had been very friendly with the oldest child, Caroline, who was a year younger than me, ever since they had arrived when I was six years old. At first we had played a lot in each others' gardens, but after a few months Caroline's mother put a stop to that, claiming that Caroline had experienced nightmares and wet the bed after playing with us and witnessing a violent family row. After that, we had to content ourselves with talking through the fence, although occasionally we were allowed to meet up under adult supervision.

My sister always maintained that during the row I had hit Caroline over the head with a stick. I have no memory of this incident – my only recollection is everyone getting angry and my brother hitting me - but I did have a furious temper and once bit my cousin Margaret when she was staying with us. My mother tried to cover the bite mark with a plaster, not realising that Margaret was allergic to them and the subsequent rash was far more obvious than the bite mark had ever been. There were also times, right up to the age of nine or ten, when all my pent up tensions, frustrations and anger would result in screaming fits, usually directed at my parents.

This was a side of me the teachers never saw, as fear made me a model pupil, although some of them were concerned about my lack of friends. One memorable day two of the children I liked invited me to play with them. For the whole day I was blissfully happy, until I overheard one of them explaining to another girl that the teacher had asked them to be kind to me as I hadn't any friends and my world promptly collapsed.

That year my school moved to a new site, further away from home and it was no longer possible for me to come home for lunch. I insisted that I would rather change schools than go back to the misery of school dinners, but when my headmaster heard of this he gave me special permission to bring a packed lunch.

The only problem with the packed lunches was that the headmaster had forbidden me to tell the other pupils that I was having them, as he didn't want it to become a general thing. Trying to hide from the others the fact that I was having packed lunches, I found nearly as stressful as having school dinners. They could not fail to notice that I was absent from the canteen (I ate in the classroom) and it was clear that I had not had time to go home. When they questioned me I could not tell a lie, yet was not allowed to tell the truth. Before long they guessed anyway and the headmaster explained that he had not meant to enforce absolute secrecy, merely to stop me from broadcasting the fact of my packed lunches unnecessarily. Things became much easier when another girl obtained permission to have packed lunches as school meals made her sick. Remembering what they were like, I'm surprised she was the only one!

Although my friend Pam was still at the school, she had by now another best friend, Angela. I still wanted to be with Pam, but she and Angela decided to ration the times I could spend with them. One consolation was that because Angela's home was in the opposite direction, I could still walk home with Pam and another girl Miriam. By walking I was able to save the tuppenny bus fare, giving a halfpenny each to Pam and Miriam and keeping a penny myself, which we would spend at a sweet shop on the way home. Of course I was honest with my mother about how I had spent the bus fare and although disapproving of the sweets, she tolerated the situation, probably glad that I was gaining some social contact.

Miriam was an Afro-Caribbean girl who not only attended my school but was also in my Sunday school class and I liked her very much. In some ways I preferred her to Pam, as she was very kind and had once defended me when all the other children had been ganging up on me. Unfortunately for me, Miriam was so popular that she had many other friends. Also, she rather despised the game which many of us played at break times.

In this game the two netball courts were designated male and female zones. If anyone strayed into the territory of the other sex and was caught, they were put in the circle in the centre which served as a prison and remained there until one of their side came and touched them. One thing I noticed with some irritation was that as soon as we managed to capture a boy, another boy would immediately rescue him, yet if a girl was taken prisoner she would often remain in the prison until the end of break, since the girls were much more cautious and fearful of being caught. Nevertheless, playing this game gave me a sense of belonging and was infinitely preferable to wandering around the playground on my own.

The inequality of the sexes was shown in other ways at school. At the infant school there had been two drinking fountains, one old and rusty, the other new and shiny. The boys claimed the new shiny fountain as theirs and made the girls use the old one. One year our class was given a box of the recently invented lego bricks. All of us longed to play with them, but the boys declared that this was a boy's toy and made sure that none of the girls got a chance even to touch the bricks. The same thing happened in the last year of junior school, when we were given chess sets, the boys insisting that this was a male only game.

Incidents like these, together with the fact that most of the children who bullied me, either physically or by name calling, were boys, made me plead with my parents to send me to an all girls' grammar school. My mother was a firm supporter of co-education, believing that many of the difficulties in her marriage arose from their mutual lack of understanding of the opposite sex, having both attended single sex schools. My sister had been sent against her wishes to a mixed grammar school where she had been badly bullied by one of the boys, to the incredulity of my parents, as he was the son of two long standing members of our church. Rachel's unhappiness and the decline in her school work meant that when we moved house, soon after my eleventh birthday, my parents finally agreed to let her go to an all girls' grammar school and said that I could go there too.

Having always found change difficult, I hated the idea of moving to a new area, even though it meant a bigger house with my own bedroom and fields and a river nearby. However, the relocation of my father's job meant that we had no option but to move. For my last term at primary school, I was sent to a school in the middle of a fairly new council estate, built to re-house people from the East end of London. On my second day, I had an argument with one girl, Tracy, who spent the rest of the term bullying me. Now I realise that Tracy had her own problems. She was in foster care as her mother was seriously ill and her father no longer around. It was hardly surprising if she resented this outspoken newcomer with her posh voice and comparatively well-off two parent family.

In order to survive at this school, I did my best to acquire a cockney accent, much to the disgust of my family, although I drew the line at copying the language. Swearing was strictly forbidden at home and my father was a stickler for correct grammar, shouting at the radio whenever the announcer made a grammatical error. He was much more patient with my errors, gently pointing out the correct grammar, but all his children have inherited his annoyance when people who should know better break grammatical rules. Some of the modern worship songs have glaring grammatical errors, such as using the word lay when it should be lie, making me want to cluck like a hen laying an egg. Instead, I usually sing the correct word loudly, rather than the one on the screen.

Although the work was boringly easy, life at this school was so stressful that I, who had cheerfully walked nearly two miles home from my old school, could barely summon up the energy to tackle the half-mile journey home from this one. Still, I consoled myself with the thought that it was only for one term and looked forward to making a new start at the grammar school in the autumn.

Chapter 3

Engulfed by Fear

When we moved house Simon stayed behind, as he was about to take his A levels and he lived in lodgings during his final term at school, before starting university in the autumn. His departure initially led to a reduction in the family rows, but the gap was soon filled by the increasing arguments between Rachel and me. My parents always seemed to take my sister's side and I felt that in my brother's absence I had inherited his role as the black sheep of the family.

There was one particular incident when I was in my early teens and we were playing carpet bowls at my uncle's house. I had beaten Rachel at this game, so I assumed that anyone who beat me should also beat her. After all, I knew from my maths that when A is greater than B and B is greater than C, it must always follow that A is greater than C. When I discovered that some of the adults who had beaten me had actually been beaten by her, I could not understand it. To my logical mind the only explanation was that they had deliberately let her win, which was unfair, so I protested loudly. The adults, knowing nothing of my confusion, merely saw a badly behaved child eaten up with jealousy. (It was only after years of watching Wimbledon, especially Tim Henman's matches, that I finally understood how someone could beat a top player one day and then be defeated by an inferior player the next.)

One thing I sensed at the time, but my parents were blissfully unaware, was that Rachel was much more skilful than Simon and I were, when it came to hiding her faults. For example, our parents insisted we went either to church or Sunday school every Sunday. Finding church boring and Sunday school childish, one Sunday I decided to rebel. I flatly refused to go and when they tried to make me, I threw such a tantrum that they were forced to give in. Afterwards I felt ashamed and thereafter went every Sunday, however reluctantly, for the rest of my childhood.

Rachel found church as boring as I did, but instead of openly rebelling, she told my parents she wanted to go to the local Anglican church as it was nearer and had shorter sermons and they consented. It was only years later I learned that on many occasions she would pretend to go to church, but instead go for a walk in the nearby meadows and spend the collection money on sweets. I couldn't help smiling when she confessed this to me, as I remembered the time when I had decided to join her at the Anglican church. Knowing that I would never agree to be a party to any deception, she had no option but to go to church with me. It must have come as a great relief to her when, after a year, I decided to return to my parents' church. Incidentally, despite her teenage rebellion, since her mid-twenties Rachel has been a very committed member of her local church, even serving as a churchwarden.

When we weren't having rows, I could still discuss most things with my sister and thanks to her and my mother I was well prepared for the onset of periods. Initially I was even quite pleased to have gained this milestone on the way to womanhood and hopefully motherhood. Though I was usually squeamish about blood, the knowledge that this bleeding was healthy and normal rather than from a wound enabled me to deal with it in a matter of fact way. One thing I did find traumatic, however, was the discovery that this was a flow of liquid totally beyond my control and my old fear of incontinence suddenly intensified.

This fear might seem unfounded for someone whose last toilet accident had been at the tender age of four, but the scornful laughter of my brother and sister was still deeply embedded in my memory. What had been embarrassing as a four year old would, now I was a teenager, be the ultimate humiliation, to be feared more than death itself.

I am sure this is the main reason why the charity that has been closest to my heart for many years is Hamlin Fistula UK, which supports a hospital in Ethiopia caring for and in most cases curing women with incontinence resulting from childbirth injuries. These poor women, in some cases girls as young as fourteen, endure days of obstructed labour, ending with a dead baby and a hole between their bladder and vagina, resulting in an uncontrollable flow of urine. For them my worst nightmare is an ever-present reality, made worse by the lack of sanitation in their homes, let alone the luxury of incontinence pads.

It is often claimed that people with Aspergers are unable to feel empathy, but this is only partially true. Whilst I am often unable to see when people are distressed, due to my difficulty in reading body language and frequently fail to appreciate the effect of my words and actions on other people, if I can relate someone's situation to something that I have experienced, even in a much smaller way, I can feel for them very deeply.

For example, when our German teacher had to leave the classroom, clearly upset by the behaviour of most of my classmates, I felt for her keenly and reproached the others for their cruelty towards her, even though I knew this would make me even more unpopular. My aunt, of whom I was very fond, had been forced to leave teaching, partly because of the behaviour of her pupils. The memory of her suffering, told to me by my mother, together with my own experiences of being bullied, enabled me to feel for this teacher and want to stand up for her.

By contrast, when my cousin Margaret came to stay with us again because her mother, who was estranged from her father, was dying of cancer, I was totally unable to grasp how she was feeling, partly because I was too steeped in my own misery, but also because bereavement was completely outside my experience.

The journey to the grammar school involved catching two buses which were usually late and sometimes cancelled. This made me extremely anxious about being late for school, especially as a cancelled bus on the very first day had made me the last to arrive and due to some error there were no desks left. In order to reduce the risk I left early and walked a mile to the bus garage, from where I could catch a bus for the rest of the way, but my dreams about being late for school persisted into my thirties and even occasionally into my forties.

In other ways the school was initially an improvement on my previous experiences. Some of the girls were quite friendly and I went a whole year without being bullied. Strangely, the bullies at the grammar school were all younger than me. In my second year two girls in the first form started bullying me and this went on for years. Even in the sixth form I was bullied by a group of third formers, who giggled as I passed by, made comments about my clothes and hairstyle or just shouted "Peanuts!" (Don't ask me why.) We were allowed to wear what we liked in the sixth form and the clothes I chose differed from the tight jeans worn by most of the others, which I found uncomfortable.

In the second year we were divided into three classes according to ability for most subjects, as well as four streams for maths and French. Finding myself in the top group for everything, for the first time I struggled with some subjects, particularly art (which I had loathed ever since an insensitive teacher had described my painting as a mess when I was six years old), creative essay writing and biology, which involved a great deal of note taking. Like most people with Asperger's I have great difficulty in writing quickly and have rarely finished the questions in an exam. Maths I still found easy, but in the A division I was at last able to work at a satisfying pace. Then an incident occurred which spoiled my enjoyment of maths for the next four years.

Early in my second year, one of the other girls asked the maths teacher if she could go to the toilet. To my horror I heard the teacher reply: "Have you no control? I don't expect this sort of thing from a second former. All right, off you go." I felt I would rather die than be spoken to like that and resolved never to ask this teacher to be excused. Of course, the knowledge that I could not leave that class meant that I invariably felt the need to, especially if it was the last class before break and the lesson which should have been my favourite was instead an ordeal until that teacher left after my O Levels.

The maths teacher's words, together with memories of my brother's taunts and the frequent references in the comedy programme *Dad's Army* to Godfrey's bladder problem, reinforced the conviction that the need to visit the toilet more often than the average person was something deeply shameful. As this need increased with the stresses of adolescence, my one thought was that this must at all costs be concealed.

What made things worse was the secrecy about such matters in those days. Although the swinging sixties had come and gone, many families, my own included, were still firmly rooted in pre-sixties ideas. My mother had impressed on me that periods were something that should not be mentioned to any man, not even my father. (Perhaps she felt the need to emphasize this because of past experiences of me bringing up inappropriate subjects in public.) None of the characters in the books I read ever needed to go to the toilet. Rachel and I used to comment to each other about the times when children in Enid Blyton books would be imprisoned for days at a time in a cave or room. Although the need for food, drink and sleep was always mentioned, other bodily needs were totally ignored.

It was no easy task trying to use the toilet in secret in a busy school. At first I found there was only a problem if one of the bullies was around, but by the time I reached the sixth form it had got to the stage that I was physically unable to go to the toilet if anyone was near, whether at school or anywhere else, including my own home. Fortunately by then I had several private study periods, during which I could slip out unnoticed, but as my A Levels approached I was forced to rely on ever stronger tranquillisers in order to survive the school day.

At the time I believed that I was the only one in the world to suffer from this problem. Amazingly, it was not until 2007 that I discovered this is a very common condition, called paruresis, affecting many thousands, possibly millions of people, most of whom suffer in silence. My own father had a mild form of the condition, finding it difficult to use a urinal when other men were around. There is now a self help group, the UK Paruresis Trust, which can help people with a problem that others find incomprehensible or even amusing.

Fear dominated every aspect of my life. At the age of ten the fear of dying and going to hell had prompted me to pray the prayer which I was told would make me a Christian and I had subsequently been baptised. Every day I conscientiously prayed and read my Bible, I gave a proportion of my pocket money to charity, attended church and did my best to lead a good and moral life. Deep down, however, although I was unaware of it, there was a growing bitterness, even hatred, towards God and towards the church which had robbed me of so much of my father's time and attention throughout my childhood.

When I was fifteen some Christian evangelists came and held a coffee bar in my town and all the young people at my church were encouraged to attend. One of the men gave such a graphic description of the scourging of Jesus that for years afterwards I was terrified to go to sleep in case I dreamed about it. Even now, more than thirty five years later, I had to stop in the middle of writing this as the emotions came flooding back. The nightmares about the crucifixion and the fear of further nightmares went on for many years and whenever anyone starts to talk about it in church I still have to beat a hasty retreat.

Any description of torture is more than I can bear and can still lead to nightmares. The Sunday school I attended between the ages of seven and eleven used to give us American leaflets, which sometimes contained stories of Christians being tortured by communists and dire warnings that the Russians wanted to conquer the world. These warnings seemed justified in the summer of 1968, when the annual treat of watching television at our grandmother's house was spoiled by the cancellation of the regular programmes to bring news of the invasion of Czechoslovakia. As I watched the Russian tanks going through the streets and heard the commentators talk of the more brutal invasion of Hungary twelve years earlier, my thoughts were: "Who will be next?" The minister of the church we attended at that time was part of a team who smuggled Bibles into Russia, risking imprisonment and possibly torture. At one time my father even talked of joining him on his next trip, much to my horror.

My history teacher at school, who in other respects was a wonderful teacher whose lessons were always interesting, seemed to revel in descriptions of tortures. One dreadful afternoon we were covering the Nazi holocaust in history followed by the crucifixion in Religious Education. How I survived that afternoon I will never know and I really appreciate my freedom now as an adult to escape these situations. Never have I had the slightest wish to return to the powerlessness of childhood and my school days.

Chapter 4

Escape into Fantasy

As my fears grew during my teenage years, so did my social isolation. This was partly due to my inability to discuss my fears with anyone except my doctor, but mainly the result of my increasing social blunders. So often I would say something which I thought was perfectly reasonable, only to find that I had caused deep offence.

PE was a constant source of anxiety as we were invariably asked to find a partner. Before each lesson I would count the number in class that day. If it was an even number I would breathe a sigh of relief, knowing that someone would have to partner me, but if it was odd I knew that however hard I tried to get a partner I would be the one left out. The teacher would then instruct me to join a pair and I would become the unwanted third. In all games, my poor co-ordination added to my unpopularity as a partner. I will never forget my first badminton lesson. Long after the others had mastered the serve, I was still vainly hitting the air, while the shuttlecock fell to the floor.

Sometimes my classmates could be quite kind to me. On one occasion when a group of younger girls ran off with my packed lunch, two of my classmates reported them to the deputy head and told her that these girls had been bullying me for some time. There was another time when one girl tried to be helpful by telling me I needed to let my hair down. I immediately replied that I couldn't as it would get in the way of my work. Although she couldn't help laughing, she did take the trouble to explain what she meant by that expression.

There was one group of five girls who would sometimes let me tag along with them, but it was clear that I was the outsider. When one of them, Hazel, had her eighteenth birthday, all the others were invited to a special meal, but I was excluded. Although any outing was an ordeal for me at that time due to the impossibility of using the toilets if anyone was nearby, the other girls were unaware of this problem. In any case, even the stresses of the outing would have been easier to bear than the pain of being unwanted. On my eighteenth birthday I had a party at home, but not one girl from school agreed to come and I ended up celebrating my coming of age with just the family.

My relationship with Hazel wasn't helped by one of my blunders during a physics lesson in the sixth form. Hazel told the teacher that she couldn't hand in her homework because she had lost her book. Puzzled, I immediately blurted out: "But you had it half an hour ago!" It was only later on I discovered that she was lying because she had not finished her work. Fortunately Hazel knew me well enough to realize that it was stupidity rather than malice that had prompted my remark, so she wasn't as angry as she might have been.

I often wondered why I was so unpopular but the only explanation I could come up with was that I was a horrible selfish person and it was my own fault. During our many rows, my sister would taunt me with "No wonder you haven't any friends!"

Increasingly, in order to deaden the pain of rejection and self hatred, I sought refuge in the world of books and, after we finally acquired a black and white set in 1969, television. At the age of eleven I discovered the *Chalet School* books, which I still enjoy reading today, despite the fact that the author, who was clearly as bad at maths as her heroine, was constantly getting people's ages wrong. With fifty eight books in the original hardback series, there was some excuse for these errors, but I would always calculate the correct age for each character. The heroine Jo, who was the first pupil, went on to marry and have eleven children, as well as adopting one child and becoming guardian to another four. This inspired me to invent a fantasy world in which I was a member of a family with eight birth children and six adopted or fostered. I was one of the foster children, Frances, who had just joined the family following her mother's death and had been warmly welcomed by the other two eleven year olds, Lesley, one of the birth children and Susan, a long term foster child.

My interest in unusual families and adoption in particular prompted me to search the library shelves for real life stories of such families. During my teens I read accounts of overseas adoptions, families with large groups of adopted children and one amazing story of a single man who brought up twelve foster children. Little did I guess when reading his inspiring story that I would one day meet his niece, herself a single adopter, who would encourage me to do the same (although I had the sense to stop at two).

Stories of children with disabilities also interested me and I read several books written by parents of children with Down's syndrome and other disabilities, some negative and depressing but others uplifting. Women's magazines also contained many interesting articles about people's lives. At the age of fourteen I first encountered the term autism through reading an article called *The small outsider*. Although this child's problems and behaviour were extreme, something about the story prompted the unspoken question "Could I be slightly autistic?"

In my early teens I was introduced to Jane Austen's books and promptly fell in love with Darcy of *Pride and Prejudice*. Like many women before and since, I was fascinated by this man, who seems so unpleasant at first yet proves to be such a hero. Looking at the story now, I believe that Darcy's real weakness was not pride, but Aspergers. Darcy himself identified the problem when he said to Elizabeth:

"I certainly have not the talent which some people possess of conversing easily with those I have never seen before. I cannot catch their tone of conversation, or appear interested in their concerns as I often see done." (Chapter 31)

Perhaps the book should be renamed *Aspergers and Misunderstanding*, although that doesn't have quite the same ring. (I was planning to write a book about Darcy and his Asperger Syndrome, but then I found that Phyllis Ferguson

Bottomer had beaten me to it with her book entitled *So Odd a Mixture: Along the Autistic Spectrum in Pride and Prejudice* (Jessica Kingsley Publishers), which confirms my theory.)

It was a television series which inspired my next fantasy world. When *The Forsyte Saga* was shown for the third time in 1970, I was completely hooked, simply lived for Friday night and bought all nine of the books, taking them all on holiday with me, despite the added weight in my suitcase. The character with whom I identified most strongly was June, who despised materialism, cared so passionately about people who were disadvantaged in any way, yet frequently made blunders in her efforts to help and was unlucky in love. In my version of the story, the character based on June and me was more fortunate, marrying a man she loved and having four children.

After two years, *The Forsyte Saga* was superseded by the television series *The Brothers* and my last and most enduring fantasy world began. It was to change and evolve over the next few years, but there was always the central theme of a secret love affair, followed by the birth of my dream child, a beautiful, intelligent little girl.

Around half way through my time at grammar school, I started walking the three miles home, tired of waiting for buses that were often late or cancelled and in which I tended to be bullied by girls from my own school and the local secondary modern. The long walk gave me a chance to slip into my dream world and recover from the stresses of the day. Night-time was another good opportunity, especially as this was a time when the fears that caused nightmares would come into my mind and the dreaming helped to drive them out, although it failed to stop the nightmares.

The ever-increasing amount of homework meant that there were few other opportunities for daydreaming in term time. Homework always took me far longer than it should have done, largely due to my perfectionism and determination to get it right. The trouble with most subjects was that there was no single right answer, unlike maths, where all you need to do is work out the solution and then you know you have finished. Fortunately, my parents strongly disapproved of doing homework on Sundays and the enforced rest gave me some time for daydreaming, as well as helping to postpone the inevitable breakdown.

Chapter 5

Help at Last

One good thing about the sixth form was being able to specialise in the subjects I liked. Pure Maths and Applied Maths were a delight, although the Pure Maths teacher did me no favours by saying, as she frequently did, in front of the class: "Fiona, you are more mathematical than the others. What do you think?"

For my third subject I would have liked to have chosen statistics, but the school didn't offer this option, so I settled for physics, since it involved quite a lot of maths. The theoretical side was not too difficult, but in practical sessions my clumsiness and lack of common sense caused quite a few problems. Once I accidentally pointed a gamma ray source at Hazel, although fortunately it was far too weak to harm her (at least I hope so) and twice I caused the water apparatus to overflow, prompting the physics master to comment that he had better wear boots next time he gave me a lesson!

Whilst the work presented few problems, the thought of the exams filled me with dread. Each paper was three hours long and even though people could ask to be excused, the fact that I would have to be accompanied meant that this was not an option for me. A few months before the exams, Simon returned home from university after an absence (apart from holidays) of nearly seven years. His return led to an increase in the rows and tensions at home and the strain of it all became overwhelming. Nothing but grim determination to get the best possible A Levels kept me going from day to day.

When taking my O Levels it had been very important for me to get better results than my sister. It was clear that my parents much preferred her personality to mine and I could not hope to compete with her in that area, but by beating her academically I could at least win their approval in one aspect of my life. Rachel had not taken any A Levels, deciding instead to train as a ballet teacher, so at first I felt a lessening of the pressure. Beating Simon was less important, since I was confident that my parents preferred me to him and always would. There was, however, a girl at church, Linda, whom my mother admired very much, clearly wishing that I was more like her. The previous year she had gained an A grade and two Bs in her A Levels which had included maths and physics. I now felt that I must beat Linda, perhaps hoping this would convince my mother that I was the daughter she wanted.

I can remember nothing of the actual exams but know that somehow I got through them. Even when they were over I could not yet relax. The need to earn some money before starting university had prompted me to apply for a holiday job in the canteen of a local factory. Looking back, it was the worst possible job for me, with the multitude of different tasks which I was unable to do quickly enough, as well as the contact with large numbers of people, quite apart from the ever present problem of having to wait until the staff toilets were deserted before using them. On the second day, when the supervisor gave me a mild ticking off over something I had failed to do, I broke down completely and had to be sent home.

After that, things happened very quickly. A psychiatrist visited my home and referred me to a clinic in London which offered me a place within a month. I hated the thought of going but knew that I could not go on living with my present burden and was too scared to commit suicide, although I frequently prayed that I might die.

When I finally entered the psychiatric clinic, I felt that I had reached rock bottom and would never lead a normal life again. It was a relief to find that most of the dozen patients on the ward were friendly and seemed reasonably sane. The majority were female, including two rather tall women who I later discovered were male to female transsexuals, but there were also two men. One was a very kind gentle man in his forties whom everyone liked. The other was younger and more reserved, although he and one of the transsexuals, Ann, had a close friendship. Most of the patients were suffering from phobias, anorexia, bulimia or depression. At least half of them had made suicide attempts, mostly overdoses, but one had slashed her wrists and another had tried to drown herself in a river.

Although the mood on the ward could be very dark, there was also the comradeship that comes from shared suffering and an atmosphere of complete acceptance. I remember Ann talking in one of the group meetings about how she felt accepted by us on the ward, but knew that it would be a different story when she went out into the world. From a recent conversation with a transsexual friend, who first tried to come out in the eighties, I fear her concerns were all too justified. This friend was subjected to insults, attacks on her house and was finally beaten up so badly she ended up in hospital. The response of the police was "It's a pity they didn't finish you off, you ****ing poof." I have never been able to understand why these vulnerable people, whose only crime is being born with the body of one sex and the mind and identity of the other, arouse such fear and hatred.

Encouraged by the friendliness and acceptance of the others, I found myself able to share the fears which I had kept secret so long, first with one other patient and later with the group, who were then able to encourage me as I progressed through the treatment programme. I had so many fears, including dogs, worms, spiders, flying insects, lifts, violence and torture as well as the toilets, that there would not have been time to treat them all, so the cognitive behaviour therapy concentrated on tackling the main one. The idea is that you are gradually exposed to the situation you most fear and learn to cope with the panic attacks, which will eventually subside. The very thought horrified me but after being told there was no alternative I finally agreed. Eight stages were involved and by the end of three weeks I reached the final stage which involved using the toilet while two men were shouting and banging on the door. Not only did I cope, but by a miracle I suddenly saw the funny side. At last I was free!

I soon discovered that I had to work hard to keep my new found freedom. Panic attacks would recur at intervals over the next few years, particularly when I was under stress, but now I knew how to deal with them. Instead of running away from the fear, I would remain where I was, try to keep calm and start counting or praying until the feelings of panic subsided. The only fear that has not been reduced to a manageable level through this method has been the fear of torture. At first I tried to make myself stay and listen, hoping to de-sensitise myself, but instead the nightmares increased. Nowadays I know it is better to slip out quietly or cover my ears, otherwise the panic rises to such a degree that I am unable to stop myself from crying out and rushing from the room.

About halfway through my stay an incident occurred which caused me some embarrassment. One of the patients, who was in a deep depression, had two regular visitors, both middle aged ladies, who usually came separately. I discovered that one of them knew my sister from her holiday job working in a shop. (Rachel was nearing the end of her training to be a ballet teacher. Although she still lived at home, I was at that time unaware that she was having her own struggles with bulimia. She was subsequently cured, without any medical help, through coming second in a beauty contest.) With my usual inability to remember a face, I muddled the two ladies up and started asking the other lady about my sister. From the way she drew back as she replied with a nervous laugh that she didn't know my sister, it was clear even to me with my limited understanding of body language that she thought I was mad.

This experience gave me valuable insight into the frustrations felt by those who are regularly misunderstood and wrongly labelled mad, stupid or drunk when in fact there is a medical explanation like cerebral palsy, a diabetic hypo or even Asperger Syndrome.

Back in 1975 the term Asperger Syndrome had not yet been invented and even those who had heard of the word autism tended to associate it with very bizarre behaviour, low intelligence, little desire to relate to other people and severely impaired speech. It is hardly surprising that the psychiatrists had to find another explanation for my difficulties and they placed the blame squarely on my parents and on religious indoctrination. The patients too, when they commented on my emotional immaturity, blamed it all on my mother for being overprotective and spoiling me. It never occurred to any of us at the time, that the overprotection might have been the result of the emotional immaturity which had a different cause, namely the developmental disorder of Asperger Syndrome.

I was only too ready to blame my family for all my problems and the resentments that had been brewing for years towards my parents, the church and God were now at boiling point. I did not hesitate to share my views with the other patients and one evening another patient called Sandra came to my room and told me her story.

When she was born the doctors weren't sure what sex she was, but they decided she was male and she was brought up as a boy and given doses of testosterone without being told what they were. Inside, however, she had always felt female and was now living as a woman and was awaiting a gender reassignment operation. In addition to this problem, she had lost her mother when a small child and had a very strict Catholic upbringing. She had been through a period of hating God, but now, when she went into a church she found a real sense of peace.

"I know you hate God now," Sandra said, "but you'll get through it just as I did and you will want to come back." These words, coming from someone who had suffered so much more than I had, gave me hope. Although she looked and sounded like a man, despite the perm (which might have been a wig) and the skirt, as I talked with her I felt I was relating to another woman, a very kind and caring woman who had found peace with God and wanted to help me to do the same.

During the last two weeks of my stay I found I was actually able to help someone else, an old lady who had been admitted following a suicide attempt. For some reason I was able to relate to her in a way that no-one else could. She talked to me a great deal about her family and her problems and for perhaps the first time I felt the joy of being needed.

Feeling the way I did about my family, I was reluctant to go home, but by the time I was discharged there were only three weeks left before I was due to go to university, which were quickly filled with preparations for my new life. Reading the Student Union handbook, I discovered that there were many clubs and societies I could join in order to make new friends. By the time the taxi took me away to start my first term, I had made two resolutions: to get involved with the voluntary work organised by the students and to have nothing to do with the Christian Union.

Chapter 6

A New Life

My resolution to keep away from the Christian Union lasted for about the first hour of university life.

After queuing up to pay my hall of residence fees, which involved braving the pickets who were trying to persuade all the students to join a rent strike, I returned to my room to unpack. As I looked at the bare grey breezeblock walls and the unmade bed, a feeling of great loneliness overwhelmed me. Much as I had wanted to leave home, the thought of being alone in a crowd of fourteen hundred students was quite terrifying.

A knock at the door interrupted my thoughts. When I opened it, a smiling girl introduced herself as a third year student living just along the corridor and said she was from the Christian Union. In my relief at seeing a friendly face, I temporarily forgot I hated Christians and said I was interested. She gave me information about a number of events, including a walk and a coffee evening as well as some more religious activities. Finally, before leaving, she invited me to call on her if I needed any help.

During the next few days I attended several Christian Union events, as well as some activities organised by the Student Union for the Freshers (first year students) and I was soon attracted to the Christians by their friendliness and sense of fun. After my long years of isolation, simple pleasures like chatting with friends over a cup of coffee meant so much. Each week several people from the Christian Union visited some old people at a local hospital, holding a short service and then talking to individual patients. Although dubious about the religious side, I was keen to get involved with voluntary work and enjoyed the visits, as well as the shared tea and singing practice that preceded each visit.

Much as I liked my new friends, my antagonism towards God was as strong as ever and I made no attempt to hide it. In fact, I quite enjoyed trying to shock the others by revealing my true feelings. I felt sure that some of the Christians secretly shared my cynicism but were not honest enough to admit it. Rather to my disappointment they appeared fairly unshockable, but after hearing my views one girl, Debbie, invited me to come to her room and talk it over with her.

I remember little of what was said that evening, but one remark made by Debbie stuck in my mind. My main argument was that God couldn't be all good when he allowed so much suffering, but I accepted that he wasn't all bad. Why couldn't he be a mixture of good and bad, like us? Debbie argued that to be both good and bad is a sign of weakness and it was impossible for an all-powerful god to be divided against himself in that way. He had to be one or the other.

There was logic in Debbie's argument that appealed to my mathematical mind, but my gut feeling was unchanged, so soon afterwards Debbie arranged for me to have a talk with the Christian Union president himself.

Clive was an extraordinary young man. At twenty, he was an experienced counsellor and spent much of his time helping people with their problems. He could stand up and preach a brilliant sermon at a moment's notice. Despite devoting relatively little time to study, he achieved an upper second in physics. In addition, he excelled at judo and several other sports. It was not long before I, along with several other girls, fell hopelessly in love with him, despite knowing that he was engaged to a girl who had just graduated from the university.

My first interview with Clive did not go well. When I told him about Sandra at the clinic and her kindness to me, he immediately said that a sex change was a sin. This led to a theological argument during which I called him a male chauvinist pig. He seemed amused rather than offended, but decided afterwards that there was little to be gained by further discussion as I had heard enough theological arguments between my father and brother to last me a lifetime. Instead, as I later discovered, he and some others concentrated on praying for me.

At this time, I found that I could tolerate most religious activities except one: I couldn't bear it when people started praying. It wasn't too bad when they were just asking God for things or praying for people who were ill (I was still doing that myself), but when they started praising him I felt sick and wanted to leave the room.

One evening, about three weeks into term, I decided to visit a friend. Just as I reached her door, she came out and told me she was going to the prayer meeting. Naturally this was the last thing I wanted to do but some strange impulse led me to go with her.

When we arrived at the bedroom where the meeting was being held, I found it packed with twenty-three people, but we managed to find a spare corner on the bed and the meeting started. One chap, Stuart, started enthusiastically praising God and as usual I felt "Get me out of here. I can't stand it." (At the time I thought: "He wouldn't pray like that if he'd suffered as I have." Months later, when he had become a close friend, I discovered that I couldn't have been more wrong.)

I decided that the next time there was a pause I would pray along the lines of: "Lord, when I hear people praising you I feel I want to be sick, but I don't want to feel like this. Please help me." When the pause came, however, I found that the prayer I had been planning had already been answered and a great load of hatred and bitterness had suddenly gone, so instead it was a prayer of thanks.

After that you couldn't keep me away from prayer meetings and a few weeks later I joined one to pray for an event being held at the same time for those with questions about the Christian faith. That evening I had been feeling quite low, yet within minutes I was caught up in an incredible atmosphere of praise and worship. Two hours later we were still having a wonderful time when Clive came in and said that as soon as he opened the door he had an overwhelming sense of the presence of God in that room. We came out as high as kites (it's a good thing the college authorities didn't see us, or they might have wanted to test us for drugs) and it was about three days before I came down to earth again.

Despite these high points I was struggling with lots of issues and was dreading going home for Christmas. I had a number of conversations with Clive, who was very kind and patient, no matter how much I argued and on one occasion disrupted the Bible study he was leading, but on the last day of term he decided it was time for some straight talking.

Among other things Clive said that God had told both him and Debbie that I was not mentally ill. At the time, I thought he was very arrogant to think he knew better than trained psychiatrists, but I now know he was right. Asperger Syndrome is not a mental illness, although the strain of living in a society filled with unwritten rules and an unspoken language which you can't understand can lead to mental health problems. Also, the inability to think quickly at times of crisis, together with hypersensitivity to certain stimuli, can lead to panic attacks and seemingly bizarre behaviour that can easily be misunderstood.

I was afraid that Clive, like so many other people, would say that my basic problem was just selfishness, but instead he said it was insecurity. He said that I was trying to find security by turning to people with my problems, but instead I needed to turn to God. I knew he was right and inwardly resolved that he would see a change when I returned the next term.

The first fortnight of the holidays I spent trying to be different but ending up rowing with my family as before. Then halfway through the holiday I decided to make a fresh commitment to follow Christ. I didn't see this as very significant at the time, and nothing extraordinary happened, but within days both I and my family noticed a big change. Instead of living by a religion imposed upon me from outside, full of rules and dominated by fear, I was in a wonderful relationship with God that was transforming me from the inside, not through my own efforts. I felt like someone who, after years of trying to move a car by sheer force, is suddenly given an unlimited amount of petrol, enabling them to drive it effortlessly. (The petrol in my tank was the Holy Spirit.)

Suddenly my eyes were opened and I began to see everyone in a new light. During my teenage years I had convinced myself that my parents didn't care about me and were only interested in my behaviour rather than my happiness. So deeply ingrained had this belief become, that there was nothing they could do to change it. Now, as the truth dawned on me that they did care very much, I was able to see evidence of their love in so many ways. My brother too, who had been an object of fear, I could now see as someone who had been badly hurt and misunderstood by his own family. As for my sister, my jealousy melted away as my happiness at university increased, causing her to look on me with envy!

Last but not least, I now saw Jesus in a different way. Previously I had pictured a cold and stern perfectionist, demanding the impossibly high standards of behaviour described in the Sermon on the Mount. Now, as I read the gospels again and started to get to know him for myself, I found a person full of warmth and humour, who could be tough with his critics but was gentle with the weak and frightened. Gradually I began to understand that the message he was aiming to get across was: "If you want to please God through your own efforts, this is how good you have to be. I know that this is impossible for you, so I have provided another way. All the bad things you have done have been punished by my death. If you trust in me I will take those bad things away and cover you with my goodness, so you will be acceptable to God just as you are."

The following summer I was baptised again, having decided that my (insurance policy against hell) conversion at the age of ten had not been genuine and my previous baptism was invalid, since Baptists only recognise baptisms that take place after a person has made their own decision to become a Christian.

On returning to university for my second term, everyone commented on the change in me. Although there would be many more battles to be fought with my fears, self pity, jealousies and resentments in the years to come, a decisive victory had been won and life, which had seemed so hopeless just six months earlier, was now filled with hope and a wonderful sense of belonging. As well as my friendships within the Christian Union, I soon made friends with some of the girls in my maths group who introduced me to the delights of discos. On my twentieth birthday early in my second year, there were so many friends crammed into my room singing happy birthday that the warden sent someone round to complain about the noise!

Chapter 7

A New Interest

The resolution to get involved with voluntary work proved much easier to keep. As well as the hospital visits organised by the Christian Union, there was a thriving Community Action Group which organised a range of activities, from visiting a nearby Young Offenders institution to helping local pensioners with odd jobs. I was keen to work with children and soon signed up for a new scheme linking individual students with a family who had a disabled child. While waiting for the link to be made, I decided to get some experience by helping at the playgroup run by the students for an afternoon each half-term for children with learning disabilities.

When I arrived at the hall where the playgroup was held, I very nearly turned and ran away. The nine children I could see were all severely disabled, some of them looked very strange, a few were making odd noises and their general behaviour seemed quite alarming. Still, I had signed up to help for the last hour and didn't like to break my word, so I stayed.

There were around ten students helping at the playgroup and before long one of them got me involved in a ball game with a teenage boy called Mark. All went well until a bad throw from me (I never was very good at ball games) resulted in Mark's glasses coming off. As he picked them up and came towards me, I thought in horror: "He's going to attack me now!"

Much to my relief Mark didn't get angry and my feelings of panic subsided. Later, as I helped at subsequent playgroups and got to know Mark better, I discovered he was a very gentle, good natured boy, far less to be feared than many mainstream teenagers. Even the most difficult children became less frightening as I got to know them. One girl, who had really repelled me at first with her misshapen head and habit of staring silently at people, proved to have the most beautiful singing voice, causing me to see her with new eyes.

In my third term I was at last introduced to my link child Vivien. She was an attractive girl whose normal appearance gave no clue to her severe learning disabilities. At thirteen she could only say a few single words and her behaviour was like that of a three year old. She was, however, friendly and good-natured and I soon became very fond of her. For the rest of my time at university I visited every Saturday for an hour or two, entertaining Vivien while her mother, whose husband usually worked on Saturdays, spent some time with her other two daughters. Singing nursery rhymes to Vivien or reading her favourite story, Goldilocks (or Liggalocks, as she called it), made a welcome change from pouring over my maths worksheets or learning my hundredth theorem. It was also good to hear that Vivien was asking for me when I was away during the holidays and looked forward to my visits.

Vivien's mother was an active member of Mencap and started to pass on to me her copy of their quarterly journal *Parents Voice.* In two of these journals there were articles about a new adoption agency, Parents for Children, set up specifically to find homes for children who because of their age or disability had previously been labelled "unadoptable". One of the articles described a campaign to find homes for babies with Down's Syndrome. I found both these articles fascinating and still have them today.

Early in my second year a group of students were invited to visit the local special school where Vivien was a pupil. The school catered for children of all ages, from two to nineteen, with a separate further education unit for those over sixteen. On visiting this unit, the teacher told us of his plans to start a youth club for his pupils and asked if we could help. Several of us volunteered and soon a fortnightly club was established. Together we would dance to music, play table tennis, darts, computer games and draughts. The pupils often beat me at computer games, which they seemed to understand better than I did. Before coming to university I had never touched a computer, or even used a pocket calculator and apart from a week long course in computer programming with an appalling lecturer, which left me hopelessly confused, I was taught nothing about computers at university.

There were four pupils who regularly attended the youth club. One of them, Mark, I already knew from the half-term playgroup. The other three all had Down's Syndrome, but had very different personalities. Gillian was extremely friendly and talkative and obviously had a crush on her teacher. Paul was also friendly, but quieter, with a great sense of mischief. One evening he hid all our college scarves and we spent a fruitless half-hour searching for them after he had returned home. In the end we had to give up and go to his house to ask what he had done with them. The fourth pupil, Derek, was rather silent and withdrawn, which just shows that not all youngsters with Down's Syndrome fit the stereotype of someone who is very friendly and outgoing.

Despite all these social activities, I still managed to fit in a reasonable amount of work for my maths with statistics degree, but my priorities had changed. On first going up to university, having achieved A grades for all my O and A levels, I had been determined to try for a first class honours degree. Within a term I decided that it was more important to have a good social life and risk getting second class honours, than make myself miserable striving for a first. On my last day at university, my tutor told me that I was on the borderline between a first and an upper second and he would let me know my degree result after I returned home. When the telephone call came, I was out at a Bible study and my brother rushed over to the house where we were meeting and shouted through the letter box: "You've done it! You've got a first!" I was touched by his genuine delight in my success, especially after he had got an upper second, but he said it was only fair that I should get a better degree than he had, as I had worked harder.

Another reason why the class of degree had become less important was that for the first time since the age of ten I was considering a career that did not involve maths. The more time I spent with young people with learning disabilities, the more I became attracted to their innocence, their lack of any pretence and their ready acceptance of anyone who showed an interest in them, instead of judging people by such superficial things as the clothes they wear or the amount of money they possess. The fact that these people were disadvantaged and undervalued by society only increased my desire to become involved with them.

As my interest grew, I started making enquiries about teacher training in special education. Such training was still in its infancy as it had only been since 1971 that children with severe learning disabilities had been given the right to receive any education. Before that, they had been classed as "ineducable". I soon found that there were only two polytechnics which offered the specialist postgraduate course and both tended to be heavily oversubscribed. Clearly I needed to gain more experience, both to increase my chance of being accepted and to confirm whether this really was the right step to take.

With this in mind I started to look for a summer job at the end of my second year in a residential home for people with learning disabilities. My initial enquiry resulted in my receiving a list of forty-five homes in the region. How on earth was I going to choose which ones to contact as I would never have time to write to them all? After talking it over and praying with two friends, Stuart and Sarah, we together selected four homes which seemed suitable.

A few days later Stuart said to me: "I think you should write to one more home. Its name keeps coming back to me. It's called The Cedars."

"The Cedars?" I said, looking blankly at him.

"Yes, it's a home for twenty girls, aged nine to forty."

For Stuart, who was famous for his bad memory, to recall such details was astonishing so I wrote to The Cedars. A few days later a reply came, offering me a job for seven weeks as an assistant matron, to fill a gap between one of the staff leaving to get married and the arrival of her successor. The letter added that this was a Christian home which had links with the local Baptist church. There had been no hint of this in the details Stuart and I had read when we had chosen the home, but somehow he had known it was the right place for me. I quickly accepted the offer and the end of July saw me making my way to the Home, filled with a mixture of excitement and very considerable trepidation.

Chapter 8

The Cedars

On my arrival at the station, I was met by a friendly girl who was a part time helper at the Home. After driving me to The Cedars she introduced me to the Home's founder, Miss Robinson, who had recently retired as Principal but lived nearby. I learnt that her successor, Mrs Gardiner, was out with some of the girls but would return shortly.

Miss Robinson gave me a warm welcome and told me all about the girls living in the Home. It was fascinating to hear how the place had been established. More than thirty years earlier, Miss Robinson had, as a single woman, adopted a baby girl who had turned out to have learning disabilities. As she had grown older, concern for her daughter's future had led Miss Robinson to found the Home so that her daughter and others like her, would have a loving Christian home after their parents were no longer able to care for them.

During my first week, I spent much of my time caring for two sisters who were staying for a fortnight's holiday. I was informed that the older girl was her parent's natural child but her younger sister, who had Down's Syndrome, had been adopted. In addition, they had a younger brother with Down's Syndrome who was also adopted. No wonder the parents needed a break!

Another person who inspired my admiration was Betty, the matron. Unfortunately our acquaintance did not get off to a very good start. When I arrived at The Cedars, Betty and some of the other staff were at guide camp with most of the girls. On their return, the first thing they wanted was a hot bath. Meanwhile I, who was off duty and unaware of their arrival, was washing my hair in the staff bathroom. When I finished and tried to unlock the door, the key broke. In the end, I managed to get out by climbing through the window onto the roof but for anyone who wasn't up to roof climbing the

47

bathroom was inaccessible. How the staff must have cursed me, although the girls all thought it a marvellous joke and kept asking me to tell them again every detail of the incident.

At first sight, Betty seemed to be just a plain, rather strict, elderly spinster but as I got to know her better my respect for her grew. Beneath her strict unsentimental exterior was a very deep love for all the girls and great wisdom in her dealings with them.

During that time Betty told me about her life, how at the age of twenty she had felt that God was calling her to work with girls with behavioural problems. She then spent the next twenty years caring for her elderly parents until finally, at the age of forty, she was at last able to pursue her calling by finding a job in a remand home.

One Sunday, soon after Betty's arrival at the remand home, she was left in charge of the girls who asked her if they could play football. Like many of her generation, Betty had been brought up to believe that it was wicked to play games on a Sunday, but somehow she realised that such a prohibition would make little sense to these girls, so she consented. Once they were tired out, she got them to sit down and explained what she normally did on a Sunday. This was the start of a regular Sunday school class. Amazingly these tough, streetwise youngsters responded positively and Betty continued working at the home for thirteen years before moving on to work with people with learning disabilities.

The twenty young women at the Home all had different personalities, ranging from extremely passive to highly volatile. Most were very friendly, but a few were more reserved. One of them, Mary, spent much of her time in a fantasy world in which she was a conductor of an orchestra. The staff tried to discourage these fantasies, feeling that they were unhealthy. They were probably right, but I felt a sneaking sympathy. I had only managed to discard my own fantasy world a few months earlier because my new life was so full and interesting. Despite the best efforts of the staff at The Cedars, Mary's life was so restricted by comparison.

The first couple of weeks at the Home I found very stressful, mainly because my duties were not clearly defined. I was not even told how much I would be paid until I had been working for five weeks, but that was the least of my worries. During the first week it wasn't clear to me when I was on or off duty and it sometimes seemed that I was just expected to see what needed doing and do it, which I found very difficult. Worst of all, it was only after arriving at the Home that I was told that the job involved quite a lot of housework. Even now, after nearly thirty years of doing my own housework, I still take much longer than most people and at that time my inexperience made me even slower. I did worry a good deal that I was failing to do my fair share of the work, but was simply unable to go any faster. Fortunately, the other staff realised that I was doing my best and although they teased me a little about the time it took to clean the bathrooms they did say that they had never known them to be so clean!

Caring for the girls in the Home was a much more pleasant part of the job and I enjoyed accompanying them on walks and escorting them on the bus to their day centre, even though the main topic of conversation in the afternoons was always what we had eaten for lunch. Supervising hair washing and other personal care also presented few problems, but one thing I did find difficult was when I was expected to persuade them to do something they didn't want to do, like their daily job in the Home or going to bed. The youngest girl, who had just entered her teens, was prone to violent temper tantrums and more than once I received scratches on my hands, yet in some ways she was easier than most of the Down's girls, who could be so stubborn that I felt like throwing a tantrum myself!

Despite the difficulties I encountered at times, I became fond of many of the girls and left The Cedars with a strengthened conviction that my calling was to work with people like them. Accordingly, I applied for the specialist teacher training course, enclosing a glowing reference from the Principal of The Cedars. Several weeks later, I was called for an interview. My hopes rose, only to be dashed a fortnight later when a letter arrived rejecting my application.

In their letter the polytechnic tried to soften the blow by stating that they had four times as many applicants as places, but this was of little comfort. For the past year I had felt increasingly convinced that this was what God was calling me to do with my life. Had I just been deluding myself? Had my tutor been right when he had told me that my plan was a criminal waste of a first class maths degree?

In the midst of my devastation over the shattering of my dream, one thing kept me going: the memory of Betty's twenty-year wait to fulfil her calling. Perhaps like her, my calling had been genuine but I would have to wait many years before pursuing it.

"Maybe" I said, when talking it over with a friend, "all this has been preparing me for having my own disabled child one day."

In the meantime, however, I had to decide what to do after leaving university. Was there any other kind of teaching I could consider? I soon learnt that the sharp dip in the birth rate in the early 1970s meant that there were few openings for teaching young children. There was of course a huge demand for maths teachers in secondary schools but I knew I could never cope with the discipline problems. The one remaining possibility was teaching in further education, so I applied to one of the teacher training colleges offering such a course and this time had no difficulty in obtaining a place.

Before starting my new course, I had the opportunity to sample something of what I had missed by helping for two weeks at a special school. Quite by accident I had learnt that my former history teacher was now teaching in a special school and when she heard of my interest she invited me to help in her classroom for the last two weeks of term. It was fascinating to see my ex-teacher in her new environment. At my school she had been a popular and interesting teacher, but very quick-tempered. Now I saw her showing an amazing degree of patience with her pupils and it was clear that she found the work very fulfilling. She told me that nothing would persuade her to go back into mainstream education.

The school was very small with just four classes and thirty five pupils. There was a friendly caring atmosphere and it seemed a happy place, but when I saw the problems encountered with some of the more difficult children I wondered whether I would have been able to manage if I had been in charge.

Whether I could have coped as a special needs teacher I will never know, but within weeks of starting my new course, I realized that I did not have the qualities needed to survive as a teacher in the mainstream world. I was too naïve and lacking in self confidence to inspire the respect that is so vital for a teacher to succeed and my perfectionism meant that lesson plans were taking far longer than they should have done, increasing the strain I was under. The sense of relief when, after discussion with my tutor it was agreed that I should give up the course, was enormous. Early in November I returned home and, after applying for several jobs, soon obtained one with an insurance company as a trainee actuary.

I had now come full circle, as this was the career I'd had in mind when first starting university, the main attraction being that it was highly mathematical, involving the calculation of insurance risks and giving financial advice on pensions and investments. The downside was the toughness of the ten exams needed to qualify. Despite the fact that nearly all the people entering the profession had a maths degree or at least a good maths A Level, I discovered that over half of them gave up and the remainder took an average of seven years to qualify. It was hardly a cheerful prospect, coming just months after I had celebrated what I thought was my last exam, but at least it was a job.

The insurance company was too far away for me to commute from my parents' home, so I found some temporary lodgings through a local church while I searched for a bedsit. Shortly after Christmas 1978 I left home once more to start a new life, alone.

Chapter 9

The Long Wait for Mr Right

Only one thing had marred those happy years at university: my lack of a boyfriend. At first it hadn't mattered. After years of social isolation I was enjoying a busy social life and making a number of close friendships and in any case, the one man I really wanted, Clive, was clearly unobtainable. Also, having just split up from my first boyfriend two weeks before starting university, I was in no hurry to start a new relationship.

I had met Colin at a party given by one of the girls at school to celebrate the end of exams. He was a decent lad who respected my views on no sex before marriage and even visited me in hospital, although his choice of gift – a book entitled *How to live with a neurotic wife* – did show a want of tact. The problem was that we had no interests in common, apart from pop music. Even there, our tastes differed and I grew tired of his attempts to educate me into liking his kind of music. Although not repelled by him, I didn't find him particularly attractive either and was quite glad of an excuse to end the friendship before starting university. I am sure this was the right decision as I was too immature and emotionally vulnerable to cope with a relationship at that time, but I wonder whether I would have been so ready to end it if I had known then how many years would pass before I would have another boyfriend.

It would have been much easier if my friends had also remained single, but one by one each found a partner, leaving me to play second fiddle. Some of them did their best to keep the friendship going and encouraged me to make friends with them as a couple, but the pain of once again being the odd one out was often intense. At one point, I was virtually the only third year student in the Christian Union without a partner.

No wonder my friends outside the Christian Union called it a marriage bureau!

What made things worse was the fact that I rarely saw these relationships coming and was sometimes even unaware that two people were going out together until someone told me. I certainly had no idea how to let a man know I was interested without making it so obvious that I scared him off. Nor could I tell whether a man was interested in me, unless he actually asked me out.

I was well aware that in social skills I lagged way behind my contemporaries. The only way I seemed to become aware of social rules was by breaking them, but at least my new friends would help me by pointing out when I got things wrong instead of just ignoring me or rejecting me completely. I blamed the years of social isolation and living in a fantasy world. Certainly, retreating into a world in which I was in control and people obeyed my rules had done little to help me relate to people in real life. Deriving most of my romantic ideas from early nineteenth century fiction also gave me few clues on how to relate to male students in the late twentieth century. Perhaps instead of Jane Austen's books I should have read the teen magazine *Jackie*.

During my final year at university, I found the lack of a boyfriend particularly hard to bear. The thought of leaving this wonderful life, saying goodbye to all my friends and facing the harsh world outside was bad enough without the added burden of being alone. Also, I felt that I was unlikely to meet so many eligible Christian men again and I knew it would be a mistake to marry someone who didn't share something as fundamentally important as my faith. In almost all churches, women outnumber men and Christian men tend to marry young, partly because the alternative, namely celibacy, has little appeal.

As expected, the first few years after leaving university were very tough. Since I was studying for exams as well as working, there was little time for a social life and the lack of a car made it even more difficult. Stuck in my lonely bedsit, I became deeply envious of my married friends. Not only did they have a companion, but with two incomes they were able to afford to buy homes of their own, instead of being forced to share a cold and filthy bathroom with six other tenants. Many times during those years I would plead with God to let me die rather than face another day alone.

There are so many awful memories of bedsit life. Quite apart from the loneliness, there was the noise of the loud music and frequent parties which would go on until the early hours, making study and sleep equally impossible. One evening I discovered that someone had been sick on the floor of the communal toilet and had not even attempted to clean it up.

Another night I was woken by the sound of the woman from the top floor flat shouting obscenities and trying to break down a door. I later found out that the reason for her drunken fury was that her partner John had started sleeping with the girl in the bedsit next to mine. Within a month John had discarded both women and moved into one of the ground floor flats with yet another girlfriend.

Perhaps the most frightening experience was when I emerged from my bedsit late one night to visit the toilet and nearly fell over a strange man lying in a drunken stupor. It later transpired that he was an illegal tenant who had to be evicted by the police.

Having spent over four months searching for a bedsit, I knew there was little point in trying to find somewhere else to live. Most of the places I had visited were even less satisfactory than my present home and there were generally at least forty people applying for each place. Nor could I have returned to my temporary lodgings. Although I had got on well with the three children, I had clashed with the landlady, a very confident, capable woman who made no secret of the fact that she thought me immature, selfish and pathetic.

The tenants of the house rarely mixed socially, but on one occasion three of them invited me to join them in a trip to the pub. Despite my initial embarrassment when they announced to their friends: "We've got someone posh with us tonight!" I was glad of the chance of some company. To my surprise, John said that he envied me my studying as it gave me some purpose and direction which his own life lacked. I wasn't so sure about that, but at least the studying offered me the hope that I might one day earn enough to be able to escape from the bedsit and buy a place of my own.

The transition to office life was also far from easy. During the first few months, the work set before me either left me totally confused or thoroughly bored. Since most of the actuarial trainees were male, for my coffee breaks I was assigned to a group of girls, most of whom had less prestigious jobs and probably resented a newcomer coming in at a higher level than themselves. I had little idea how to relate to these girls whose main topics of conversation were gossip and their boyfriends. To them it was incredible that anyone could exist without a boyfriend and it was clear that they thought I was very weird.

One of the girls, Beverley, was quite friendly, even inviting me to her home for a meal. Like me, she had become a Christian at university and she had also experienced life in a bedsit, although it had not taken her long to find a boyfriend and she married him a few months after I started work. The following year, she left to have a baby and once she had gone the other girls became more open in their hostility, forcing me to seek other companions for my coffee and lunch breaks.

Looking back, I realize that I made many blunders which the girls probably interpreted as veiled insults. Once, when everyone was commenting on one girl's new hairstyle, my remark was: "Yes, I think I'll like it when I get used to it." Now I realize how insulting that must have sounded, but at the time I was merely trying to express my honest opinion which was that I thought it was nice, but like anything new, I needed time to get used to it. Mind you, I couldn't win even if I said something pleasant about their clothes or hairstyle as they would often draw back and say: "We'll have to watch

55

this one", implying that I fancied them, since my lack of a boyfriend meant I must be gay.

This experience of rejection was repeated more than once in this particular job. Later on I drew some comfort from the discovery that at least three other girls working for that company had also suffered from the unkindness of colleagues, suggesting that the fault was not entirely mine, but at the time each rejection further demolished the fragile self esteem and confidence I had gained at university.

At one time three women saw me having lunch alone and invited me to join them in future. I accepted gladly, but a few months later two of them told me that the third woman, Christine, had taken a violent dislike to me because I had dared to argue with her extreme right wing views. They admitted to me that Christine was a very difficult woman and they often disagreed with her opinions, but kept silent in order to keep the peace. Trying hard not to show them how upset I was, I thanked them for being so honest with me and asked if they, like Christine, would prefer not to have lunch with me in future. After hesitating, one of them said: "To be honest, you haven't really much in common with us. I'm married, Kim's engaged and Christine is living with someone. You haven't even got a boyfriend." Little did she know how those words hurt me as they confirmed the social stigma of my singleness.

One thing that kept me going during this time was the friendship shown by people at the large Anglican church I had joined when I moved into the area. There was a group for people of my age that met every Sunday evening and the girls in that group gave me a warm welcome. Some of the older people in the church also offered friendship and the occasional meal.

A year after I joined the church, the four hundred people in the congregation were allocated to a number of small groups called Caring Groups. Some of these did little more than meet up for Bible studies and the occasional social event, but my group certainly lived up to its name. The leaders, Richard and Jean, were always willing to provide a listening ear when the loneliness got too bad or when a crisis arose and all the members of the group tried to help each other in practical ways. I sometimes babysat their two daughters of whom I became very fond.

When I first joined the young people's group at church, there were a number of single men. Not surprisingly, more than once I fell in love with one of the men, only to suffer the inevitable heartache when they found a girlfriend. One man who had been very friendly with me for several months, suddenly started going out with my best friend, who was too embarrassed to tell me. A few weeks earlier, I think he did try to prepare me by telling me that there was a girl he was interested in, but since he mentioned no names, I misunderstood and thought he was talking about me. Somehow, my friendship with both of them survived this blow and when I saw some of the difficulties they experienced in their relationship over the next few months, I began to think that I had had a lucky escape. (In all probability, so had he.)

With life again becoming so difficult and lonely, the temptation to escape once more into a fantasy world was intense, but this time I tried to resist it, knowing that the fantasies would make it even harder for me to learn how to live in the real world. I soon found that, like an alcoholic who returns to drink after being dry for more than a year, I was addicted to my fantasies. In some ways this addiction was harder to fight than a drink problem. At least you can reduce the temptation to drink by keeping no alcohol in the house, but where can you escape from your own mind? After a few years, I decided to write down the fantasy as a short novel in an attempt to get it out of my system and then put it behind me. At the same time life began to improve, making it easier to face reality.

After three years of studying, I completed the first half of my actuarial exams and was at last able to afford a place of my own. Within three days of starting my search, I found the perfect flat, just within my price range and opposite the church, close to my friends. Three people from my Caring Group spent a whole day helping me move and cleaning my new flat. The bliss of having my own front door, with a bathroom and telephone all to myself, can hardly be described. Although I had entertained a number of people in my bedsit, it was certainly much easier now that I had a proper flat and did not have to ask people to sit on the bed to eat their meals.

A few months later, I told my vicar of my interest in special needs and asked if he knew a family who would be glad of some help. He introduced me to a divorced lady with two little girls, aged three and four, the older of whom had learning disabilities and I started looking after them each week while their mother did her shopping. This was the start of a long and happy friendship with two delightful children and the following year I became their godmother. Soon afterwards, I made friends with a young widow, Sharon, and used to care for her baby daughter while she helped with the local guide company.

The next year brought a new interest as my sister, who had married two years earlier, announced that she was expecting a baby. The whole family was delighted and I loved being an aunt to her son Edmund and later his sister Catherine. Even so, my pleasure was marred by the knowledge that although they were so precious to me, to them I could never be more than one of their many visitors whom they enjoyed seeing but could quite happily live without. The longing for a child of my own, who would really need me and depend on me, was growing all the time and the ache of childlessness was getting ever harder to bear. The frequent birth notices from my university friends only added to the heartache and whenever anyone left work to have a baby, I wondered whether it would ever be my turn.

By this time, life at work had improved significantly. In 1983 I had changed jobs and found my new colleagues much more friendly and accepting. Perhaps part of the reason was the change in me, due to the harsh lessons learnt in my previous job, as well as the attempts I had made to improve my social skills through reading such books as *How to win friends and influence people* by Dale Carnegie. Whatever the reason, I found new interest in my career and gained the incentive I needed to continue with my studies, despite having failed both my exams in the last two years. The early exams had involved a great deal of maths and statistics which had presented few problems, but the last four required a considerable amount of essay writing and once again my slowness meant that I could never finish a paper in time, resulting in repeated failures.

Most of the men in my age group at church had now married, but whenever I went on holiday there was the hope that I might meet someone special. In 1984, on a drama holiday at a Christian centre, I became friendly with one man, Graham, and my hopes rose when he asked for my address. During the next few months, we exchanged several letters and he visited me twice. Unfortunately, I probably scared him off by appearing too keen. His final letter, in which he said that he only wanted friendship but feared I wanted more, was painful to receive, but I appreciated his honesty in telling me directly how things stood, instead of just leaving me in suspense by ceasing to answer letters. I did, however, feel it was rather unnecessary for him to send me a Christmas card ten months later in which he told me that he had met someone else.

A few months after this disappointment my friend Sharon, who had just got engaged, tried to pair me off with a Christian friend of hers, arranging for us to meet on a group outing to the zoo. She thought that we would get on well, as we had similar personalities. Rather too similar, I soon decided, seeing some of my own faults glaringly reflected in him. Meanwhile, he told Sharon that he had never been able to fancy a woman with glasses, despite wearing them himself and the friendship soon died a natural death.

Soon afterwards, at a New Year holiday at a Christian centre, I met Luke. We had both joined a drama workshop and were cast as joint narrators for the sketch to be performed on the final evening. The rehearsals brought us together a good deal and I enjoyed his company immensely. Luke had a great sense of humour (something Sharon's friend had sadly lacked) and we had many laughs together, as well as more serious talks. One mealtime, we were so engrossed in conversation that the other people on our table had to ask us to stop talking and eat our chilli con carne – they wanted their pudding!

I was sharing a room with six other women in their twenties and thirties, so for the last evening we performed our own sketch based on the seven dwarves, showing the seven of us coping with the cramped conditions in our room. The punch line was: "And you single girls thought you didn't like living alone!"

Afterwards, back in our room, all seven of us talked late into the night. On the surface we were all successful singles with interesting careers and no obvious personality problems, but a different picture emerged as we shared the heartaches and frustrations of the single life. One of the speakers at the conference, a middle aged lady whose main mission in life was to promote singleness as a positive option, would have been horrified to hear us, especially after the excellent talk she had given on this subject just two days earlier.

Before the holiday ended, Luke asked for my address, so I returned home full of hope. This was somewhat dimmed when more than a month elapsed before receiving a reply to my letter. Each evening I would rush home from work in eager anticipation, quickly followed by bitter disappointment when once more faced with an empty doormat, or just a collection of bills.

Eventually Luke did write and told me he was facing probable redundancy. This seemed to explain his silence and hope returned. After seven months, however, during which we had only seen each other once, I forced myself to face the truth. We had already arranged a second meeting the following month, so to forestall the rejection which I sensed was coming, I wrote to Luke, explaining my feelings and saying that since I believed he didn't return them, it would be better to cancel his visit. In the letter I stressed that any hurt I felt was not his fault as he had never knowingly given me false hopes. His reply, even though it confirmed my fears, came as something of a relief. Anything was better than the wild hope, alternating with despair, which had dominated the past few months. There was also the faint comfort that although I had failed to win his love, his letter showed that the way I had dealt with the disappointment, without bitterness or blame had at least earned his respect.

It was time to take stock. In a few months time I would be thirty and felt that the chances of meeting the right man were now very low. At the same time, I was well aware that marriage had its trials and was increasingly wary of marrying the wrong person. Also, life as a single woman had improved considerably over the years. I could now drive and had just bought my first car. I had a comfortable home, several good friends, two lovely goddaughters and a delightful nephew. Moreover the end of the exams was now in sight – I had only one left to pass. Having now experienced over seven years of independence, I had become used to a freedom that would have to be sacrificed in marriage.

Besides all this, I was tired of getting hurt, tired of giving my heart to those who didn't want it. Surely the time had come to forget about marriage and accept lifelong singleness? There was just one major drawback – the longing for a child of my own was stronger than ever.

Chapter 10

A New Hope

Shortly after receiving Luke's final letter, I heard of a scheme run by a local charity, linking volunteers to families who had a child with special needs. Each volunteer was matched with a family and would care for the child for short periods in the volunteer's own home. This sounded just what I was looking for: a close relationship with a child who really needed me, so I contacted the charity.

My interest in people with learning disabilities had not waned over the years of studying. On a recent holiday, one of the families had an adorable little boy of nearly three with Down's Syndrome and I had so wished that he was mine. Any temptation to self pity over my childlessness had, however, been checked by the sight of one of the other guests, a man with no arms due to thalidomide, who seemed to accept his disability without bitterness and managed to perform many tasks, including feeding himself, with his feet. To paraphrase an old saying: "I cried because I had no child to hold in my arms, but then I saw a man with no arms and I stopped crying."

On another occasion, I had seen a short film on television, showing some young people with learning disabilities working at their day centre and enjoying a trip to the seaside, accompanied by the Hollies song *He ain't heavy. He's my brother*. As I watched and listened I felt a strange yearning and thought: "That is what I am meant to be doing."

When the organiser of the Link Scheme, Diane, came to visit, she explained that all prospective volunteers, or Link Parents, had to undergo an assessment. This involved interviews and training sessions, a written application, two references and a police check. The whole process was expected to take a few months, but in my case it extended to over a year, due to a series of mishaps. In the first place,

Diane left her job in the middle of my assessment and by the time her successor Eileen was appointed several months later, my papers had been lost. Wearily I completed a second application form and prepared for a further wait. There was another short delay as a change in procedures meant that they had to repeat the police check. Altogether, they must have carried out three police checks on me, which did seem a little excessive for someone whose worst crime had been parking on a single yellow line for five minutes and I hadn't even been caught!

During this long waiting period, I took my last exam for the third time and I finally managed to pass. Two of the men in my department qualified at the same time so there were great celebrations that day. The relief of not having to face any more exams was immense, although the increased work pressures, together with the responsibility of managing a team of actuarial trainees and going to client meetings, ensured that the job remained stressful. Soon afterwards, the directors invited all the newly qualified actuaries to lunch and asked us to describe how we hoped our careers would progress. I gave the answer I assumed they expected, but felt I was living a lie, pretending to be an ambitious career woman when inside I knew that my only ambition was to be a mother.

In June 1988, nearly two years after my initial enquiry, Eileen telephoned to say that she had a prospective link with a baby boy with Down's Syndrome. Having previously been told to expect a school age child, I was thrilled to be linked with a baby. Eileen then went on to tell me that this baby, Adam, was the younger of two boys, both with Down's Syndrome, who had been adopted by a single woman called Lindsey.

After hearing this, I couldn't wait to meet the family. The dream of adopting a child with a disability had been growing in the back of my mind for so many years, yet until now it had seemed like one of my fantasies that had little hope of becoming a reality. In the first place, what adoption agency would approve me as a single woman, especially one who had once had a breakdown? Secondly, how would I manage financially as I would have to give up work? Lastly, was I strong enough emotionally to cope with a disabled child?

When I met Lindsey she was keen to encourage me to consider adoption and soon disposed of the main objections. She explained that most adoption agencies now welcomed single women who were prepared to accept a child with a disability, or an older child with emotional problems. When I explained about the breakdown, she told me that many social workers recognised that those people who had survived difficult experiences often made better adopters than those whose lives had been relatively trouble free.

Lindsey also explained that adoption allowances were available for people on low incomes adopting children with special needs, as well as disability benefits. Since these benefits were counted as the child's income, the adopter could still claim Income Support and have their mortgage interest paid. Of course, I would still be facing a substantial drop in income from my present salary, as I was by now a high rate taxpayer, but that mattered little. For some years my income had been far more than I needed or even wanted, since I had no interest in designer clothes or other status symbols like expensive cars or a big house. My parents had always been content with a simple lifestyle and as their income increased with my father's promotions, they just gave more away to people in need. Their pleasure in doing this, although they seldom spoke of it and kept their giving as secret as possible, gave me an example I was keen to follow.

One potential problem remained: the doubt over whether I would be able to cope with the practical and emotional demands of single motherhood. Lindsey was clearly managing very well with her two and was even looking for a third child, but she seemed to be a much stronger and more confident person than I could ever be. Clearly I would have to think it over very carefully, but in the meantime, what better preparation could I have than being a Link Parent?

Before the link could be approved, Lindsey and I had to arrange a few meetings so that Adam and I could get to know each other. I quickly became fond of Adam who was a beautiful baby with a sunny personality. The only unattractive thing about him was his frequent vomiting. Still, I had become used to that with my niece Catherine who had been born the previous year, so I asked my sister to send me a good supply of her old bibs.

Just before the bibs arrived, Eileen asked to come and see me. She then explained that although Lindsey was happy for me to be linked with Adam temporarily, in the longer term she wanted him to have a link family with two parents and other children. The panel had refused to approve a short-term link, feeling that it wouldn't be fair on me, so it had all fallen through.

This was a sharp disappointment and for weeks afterwards I couldn't bear the sight of the great mound of bibs which my sister had sent for Adam. Still, despite dashing my hopes as a Link Parent, Lindsey had left me with the hope of something even better – a child who would become my own.

A few weeks before meeting Lindsey I had joined a pen friendship club for single Christians. Over the past few years, particularly since my heartache over Luke, I had tried so hard to come to terms with the single life. I had read numerous books on the subject, attended a weekend conference designed to help Christian single women make the most of their lives as singles, received prayer and counselling, as well as concentrating on my career and other interests, but nothing could change the deep longing to love and be loved. To deny these longings felt like killing a part of myself.

When my vicar had first suggested that I should join a Christian dating agency, six years earlier, my attitude had been one of revulsion, but since then my views had undergone a change. I knew several people who had tried this route, one of whom was happily married as a result. I suspected that others, who despised such methods, sometimes waited in vain for the right husband and then married someone quite

65

unsuitable through desperation. Having experienced the guessing games and uncertainties involved in my previous friendships with men, I appreciated the directness and honesty of openly admitting that you were looking for someone.

The agency I joined sent a list of all the members of the opposite sex, with brief details of each, including age, location, occupation, church denomination, interests, dislikes and the type of person they wished to meet. Members were expected to follow Christian standards of celibacy before marriage. They were also encouraged to contact several different people and build up a number of friendships until they felt they had met someone special with whom they wanted a one-to-one relationship.

I was somewhat sceptical about the type of men who would join such a club. With the number of single Christian women greatly exceeding the number of men, I thought that any Christian man unable to find a girlfriend in the usual way must have something very wrong with him. Perhaps because my expectations were so low, I was pleasantly surprised. During my year of membership I met ten men and corresponded with several more. None was actually repulsive and one I found really attractive, both in looks and personality, but perversely this was the date where everything went wrong.

The restaurant where we met had been my suggestion, being one in which I had enjoyed some good meals with friends. That evening, however, first my companion found that his chicken was badly underdone, then the cream curdled in his coffee and finally, when he received the bill, he found that he had been overcharged. I was most impressed by the calm, polite yet firm way with which he dealt with these irritations, but wondered aloud whether the waitress was a discarded girlfriend out for revenge! Anyway, that was the last I saw of him, which was rather a shame, but not altogether surprising.

From the start, I was determined not to take these dates too seriously, just enjoy the friendships and take one step at a time. The new hope I found soon after joining the organisation, that I might be able to gain a family by adoption even if I didn't marry, made this much easier. Doubtless this more relaxed attitude helped to attract men to me and for the first time in thirteen years I found myself having to turn men down who were getting too serious about me.

It was a strange and illuminating experience to see in some of these men, the very things that had probably put men off me in former years. Self pity was the biggest turn off, closely followed by obvious desperation for a partner. When one man talked of wanting to marry me on the second date, (which I had already decided would be our last), I just wanted to turn and run. I have since wondered whether my chief attractions were my highly paid job and British passport, since he had originally come from overseas and his obvious materialism had been the first thing that had put me off.

There were a couple of other men whom I liked well enough as friends, but whose emotional immaturity (combined with a lack of physical attraction due to obesity), made it impossible for me to consider them as anything more. Having seen real life examples of the misery of a marriage in which the wife is unable to respect her husband, I knew that the words of Mr Bennett in *Pride and Prejudice* still rang true:

"I know that you could be neither happy nor respectable unless you truly esteemed your husband, unless you looked up to him as a superior." (Chapter 59)

Doubtless there are many women who are able to feign a respect that they do not feel in order to keep their husbands happy, but for me that was impossible. If I could not find and attract a man who inspired my respect as well as my affection, it was better to remain single.

When my membership was due for renewal at the end of the year, I let it lapse in order to concentrate on my search for a child, but I found the experience more effective than any book or seminar in reconciling me to the single life.

Chapter 11

The Search Begins

In the months following my meeting with Lindsey, I read all the books and articles I could find on adoption and Down's Syndrome, while I considered my next move. It was one thing to long for a baby, but quite another to take on a child who would never be fully independent. How would I cope as the child grew into a teenager and then an adult? Was it madness to think I could cope at all with the demands of single parenthood? Despite all the progress I had made in the years since my breakdown, I knew I was still prone to anxiety and found change difficult and this was a change of monumental proportions. Sometimes I felt like the accountant in the Monty Python sketch who said he wanted to be a lion tamer. (One of the classic definitions of an actuary is someone who found accountancy too exciting!)

Alongside my concern over my child's future as an adult, there was the fear that the child would never grow up, as I remembered all the stories I had heard and read of Down's children who died young. At least the books I read now provided some reassurance on this point. I learnt that medical advances in recent years gave Down's children a very good chance of surviving at least until middle age, unless they were born with a serious medical condition such as a severe heart problem. The improvements in education also meant that many children with Down's Syndrome were now achieving much more than in former years. My own memories of the young people I had known and my enjoyment of their company, in some ways preferring them to mainstream teenagers, was another source of encouragement.

On the other hand, I was aware that the degree of learning disability varied considerably from one Down's person to another. This was brought home to me one day when I was out shopping and saw two young women with Down's

Syndrome. The first was in the supermarket with her elderly mother, made noises instead of talking and was rocking backwards and forwards looking thoroughly miserable. By contrast, the other young woman was by herself in the library, busily scanning the bookshelves for the books she wanted. My own experiences, together with the books I had read, suggested that the second woman was more typical of a person with Down's Syndrome nowadays, but there were no guarantees.

Adoption would clearly be a giant leap of faith. In the end, as with all decisions, I decided that only one thing really mattered: was this what God wanted me to do? If it was, he would enable me to cope and find fulfilment in the task, but if it wasn't, I could end up ruining another life as well as my own.

My own sense of calling that I had known for the past twelve years to work with people with learning disabilities, together with the growing longing for a child, were powerful indicators that this was the right move. In addition, unlike the other routes to becoming a single parent, which I had been tempted to consider, I could see no moral objection to the plan. Whilst it was true that any children I adopted would have no father, if I didn't adopt them they could easily end up with no parents at all. As a single woman, I knew that I would only be considered for a child deemed "hard to place" and was unlikely to be chosen if a suitable couple came forward for that child.

After several months of research and discussions with close friends and family, who despite understandable reservations were willing to offer their support, I decided the time had come to take the plunge. I would apply to adopt, and trust that if it was the right decision I would be successful, but if it wasn't, then I would either be prevented from adopting, or would realise my mistake before it was too late.

As a first step, I contacted British Agencies for Adoption and Fostering (BAAF), who sent me some useful leaflets, a list of adoption agencies and details of an adopters self help organisation, now called Adoption UK. Both BAAF and Adoption UK publish newsletters containing profiles of children needing new families. Quite a number of the children were from ethnic minority or mixed race backgrounds, but I had already learnt that as a white person I would have little chance of being considered for a non-white child. Most of the other children featured were over the age of eight. Although few details were given about their backgrounds, it was apparent that many had suffered considerably from neglect and abuse before coming into care and had severe emotional problems. Seeing all the photographs of these children who were so desperate for someone to love them made me wish I had the special qualities needed to care for a troubled child, but I knew that task was beyond me.

Among all the profiles of older children, it was encouraging to see details of two Down's babies needing a home. Since the magazine had first been issued several weeks earlier, I knew that it was likely adopters had already been found for them, but seeing their profiles gave me hope.

Clearly, the first thing I needed to do was find an adoption agency willing to assess me. It seemed sensible to approach first an agency linked with the Church of England, since the fact that I was then attending an Anglican church should be a point in my favour. The response to my initial enquiry was far from encouraging. I was informed that they already had two couples who had each been waiting two years for a baby girl with Down's Syndrome, although they would not have needed to wait so long for a boy. I had already discovered that most adopters had a preference for girls, which unfortunately I shared. On hearing that the preparation classes for prospective adopters would be at a time that would mean driving on the M25 in the rush hour, I decided it would be wiser to try an agency nearer home.

At this point, I heard from Lindsey again. One evening, towards the end of February 1989, she telephoned to say that she was adopting a third child, one of the Down's baby girls I had seen in the adopters' magazine and wanted me to be her Link Parent. I was more than happy to accept and told Lindsey of my plans to adopt as well. Immediately, she invited me to visit and talk it over.

When I saw Lindsey she was full of encouragement, reassuring me that although Down's babies were becoming increasingly popular, families were still needed. The fact that she had just been offered her third child, despite being single and needing an adoption allowance, suggested that I did have a chance. The important thing was to get myself assessed by an agency as soon as possible, since this usually took at least six months and no child could be placed with me until I was approved.

One thing Lindsey said that night proved to be prophetic: "Your child has probably already been born and is out there somewhere waiting for you."

The next day I wrote to another adoption agency nearer my home. A few weeks later, a reply came from one of their social workers and it was arranged that he would visit me on 14 April.

Meanwhile, Lindsey was being introduced to her new prospective daughter Philippa. Within a few weeks, however, Lindsey reached the painful conclusion that her family was not the best one for this little girl. Philippa was a very passive baby who would need a great deal of attention and stimulation which Lindsey did not have time to give and she seemed frightened of Lindsey's two boys. Having talked it over with Philippa's foster mother, both of them felt that Philippa would be better placed with someone who had no other children, in fact someone like me.

Lindsey suggested I contacted Philippa's social worker immediately to enquire about her. Since it would be a couple of months before her details could appear again in the adopter's magazine, I would have the advantage of applying first. The only snag was that by the time I managed to get myself approved for adoption, another family might be found. Still, it was worth a try.

Before Philippa returned to her foster home, Lindsey invited me to meet her. Unlike Adam, she was not a very attractive child to look at, partly because of a squint, but she was a sweet little girl who needed someone to love her. As I held her in my arms I felt sure that I could soon become attached to her, if given the chance.

Later that day I wrote to Philippa's social worker, expressing my interest. Two weeks later, on receiving no reply, I telephoned. The social worker informed me that they were planning to feature her again in the next magazine and would then consider my application, along with any others. This was not particularly encouraging but still left room for hope.

Chapter 12

"I don't like Thursdays"

On the evening of Thursday 13 April, I was just finishing cleaning my flat and looking forward to my favourite radio programme when the telephone rang.

"Who can that be?" I thought. "I hope they won't be too long, as I don't want to miss *The Archers*". It was my mother.

"Are you sitting down?" she asked.

"Yes," I replied, puzzled.

"Your father's been in a bad road accident. He's dead!"

"I don't believe it," I kept saying, dazed with shock, but it was all too true. Apparently, he had been cycling from the office to the church to do some organ practice in his lunch hour and at the traffic lights he had either fallen off or been knocked off and ended up under a lorry. The only comfort was that death must have been immediate.

When I finally put the telephone down, forgetting all about *The Archers*, I mechanically finished cleaning the flat and then called some friends who immediately came round. Ironically, only the day before, I had attended the funeral of a work colleague and had felt terribly awkward talking to her son, who had worked for us the previous summer, because I couldn't begin to imagine what he was going through. Now, as I saw the same embarrassment in my friends, I knew only too well how it felt to be bereaved. Nor did it matter that my friends didn't know what to say. For me the fact that they were there and the knowledge that they cared was enough.

My mother, knowing of my appointment with the social worker the next day, had stressed that there was no need for me to come to see her until the weekend as my aunt was with her and my sister lived nearby. Accordingly, despite a largely sleepless night, I went to work as usual in the morning, then returned to my flat to await the social worker's visit.

When the social worker Mr Brown arrived, at first I made no mention of what had happened, only bringing it up when he started asking how I would cope if my adopted child died. I hoped that the way I was coping despite such a devastating blow would be seen as a sign of strength, but it had the opposite effect. Not realising how much of my calmness of manner was due to being numb from shock, Mr Brown concluded that I was a cold person who had little feeling for my father.

Mr Brown then proceeded to ask detailed questions about my life history. He was clearly very concerned about my breakdown at age eighteen and questioned me closely about the family conflicts and other factors that had led up to this crisis. I replied with my usual frank honesty.

I was also told that Down's babies, particularly girls, were very popular and I had little chance of adopting one under the age of two. When I told Mr Brown about Philippa he was pessimistic about my chances, but understood my urgency to be assessed.

On the positive side, Mr Brown acknowledged my experience and obvious commitment and agreed to start an assessment.

On returning to my mother's home the next day, I learnt that the night before he died my father had attended a midweek meeting at church, in which the discussion had been about heaven. My father had joined in with enthusiasm saying what he was most looking forward to in heaven, little realising that he only had a few hours to wait. Whilst this was a huge comfort, it was still hard to pick up the television magazines and see how as usual he had circled all the programmes he had been intending to watch that weekend.

Over the weeks that followed, I helped my mother sort through various financial papers and discovered for the first time the full extent of my father's generosity to people in need. Whilst discussing everything with my mother, he had kept it as secret as possible from everyone else. Having known someone who had discovered that her father was a bigamist after his death, it was good to reflect that my father's only secret was such a positive one.

During this time I had a number of dreams, all of which strengthened my conviction that my father was safe in heaven. In one of them he returned to us for a brief visit. Although he refused to tell us anything about heaven, there was an aura of peace surrounding him. In another dream, I saw him being welcomed into heaven by Jesus, who healed him of all the hurts he had carried since early childhood.

My mother, after the initial shock, was coping well. In the past she had always made a point of befriending lonely people so she already had many single and widowed friends, unlike many new widows whose only friends are married.

One Thursday afternoon, exactly two weeks after my father's death, my boss informed me and the other two assistant actuaries that he was being transferred to another department. Apparently, the senior directors had wanted him to move at once, saying that we would have to carry on as if he had been run over by a bus, an attitude that struck me as particularly heartless after what had happened. They had eventually agreed that his move could be staggered over a few months. Even with this concession, there would be a substantial increase in our already heavy workload.

The following Thursday brought a further shock when my dentist informed me that an X-ray had revealed an abnormal growth in my jaw.

"Could it be cancer?" I asked fearfully.

The dentist was unable to rule this out and said he would refer me to a specialist. Faced with this fear, all my other troubles faded into insignificance as I contemplated the possible loss of my ability to speak or eat normally. Fortunately a telephone call to a dentist friend soon reassured me that as a young non-smoker my chances of this type of cancer were very small. Some time later the specialist confirmed that the growth was almost certainly harmless. He added that this type of growth was rare in white people but more commonly found in Afro-Caribbeans.

On receiving this information I fleetingly wondered whether I could use it to convince the adoption agency that I must have some Afro-Caribbean blood, notwithstanding my blue eyes, fair skin and light brown hair that only curled with the aid of a perm. I would then be allowed to adopt one of the many mixed race children in need of homes, who were often left languishing in care because of the strict same race policy now followed by most agencies, which generally prevented white people from adopting them. Sadly, I decided that I was unlikely to be believed.

My adoption assessment was now under way, starting with a detailed application form, yet another police check, a medical examination and two references. After this, I had two further interviews with Mr Brown, who probed deeply into my background and character in an attempt to discover whether I was fit to adopt.

During this period I visited an ex-colleague, Alison, who had adopted two children and discovered that she had also been assessed by Mr Brown. She warned me (too late) that Mr Brown tended to seize on any negative thing you admitted and magnify it out of all proportion. He had, however, eventually recommended her approval for adoption, but she had two advantages over me: not only was she married but she was also Asian and there is a shortage of Asian adopters.

Despite the doubts Mr Brown was expressing, the fact that the assessment was continuing gave me grounds for hope. After his visit in June, however, Mr Brown broke his leg and had to postpone his next visit until the end of August.

In the meantime I was searching for a house, since my flat was unsuitable for a child. Within a few weeks I found the ideal home, a three bedroom terraced house with a small garden in a quiet cul-de-sac, large enough for a family, yet cheap and easy to maintain. The position was also ideal, near the church and the shops, with a duck pond and park nearby. There was just one big snag: the major housing slump of 1989 meant that it was proving impossible to sell my flat.

My mother, who had received a lump sum from my father's pension fund, offered to lend me the money to buy the house. At first I hesitated, but eventually, faced with the prospect of losing the house unless I made an offer quickly, I decided to take the plunge. The purchase went ahead smoothly and the completion date was set for Thursday 31 August, the day of my next appointment with Mr Brown.

All this time I was still cherishing the hope that I might be allowed to adopt Philippa. When her profile appeared in the next adoption newsletter, I reminded her social worker that I was still interested and that I was now halfway through my assessment. Although I knew that statistically speaking my chances of success were slim, hope still burned until one day in the middle of August when a letter arrived from Philippa's social worker. In it, she said that they had drawn up a shortlist of applicants and I wasn't on it.

This was a bitter end to all those months of hope and suspense. When one of my goddaughters said to me a few days later: "I expect God has got another baby for you," it was of little comfort. Like a woman who has miscarried, I needed first to grieve for the child I had lost.

Nevertheless, there was some encouragement from the fact that my assessment was continuing. Once approved, I would have a better chance of being chosen for a future child. Before his visit, Mr Brown wrote to say he would be bringing his supervisor with him. Alison had told me that the agency always brought in another social worker for a second opinion towards the end of the assessment, so I saw this as a hopeful sign.

On the morning of Thursday 31 August, I collected the keys to my new house, quickly inspected my new home to check that all was well, then hurried back to my flat to welcome Mr Brown and his supervisor. Whilst making them a cup of tea, I told them enthusiastically about the new house, assuring them that it was ideal for children. Suddenly, without warning, they dropped their bombshell: they were rejecting my application.

I stared at them, devastated. Yet again, all my hopes and dreams had come crashing to the ground.

Chapter 13

"Don't Give Up!"

The day after my rejection by the adoption agency I felt too depressed and defeated to go to work and spent the day quietly with my mother, who had come over on hearing the news. With a heavy heart I showed her my "perfect family home", which seemed so big and empty now. I also phoned Lindsey, who urged me not to give up and invited me to come and see her again.

During the following two weeks I was kept too busy to dwell much on what had happened. As well as moving house, I had to attend an actuaries' conference and the inquest on my father's death which was held, predictably, on a Thursday. Hard as the inquest was for us, it must have been even worse for the lorry driver, although the conclusion was that no-one was to blame for the accident. Afterwards my mother gave the lorry driver a letter expressing sympathy for what he must have been through and reassuring him that we knew it was not his fault. She added that we were sure my father was in heaven. The lorry driver's reply, together with the flowers he sent, showed how much he appreciated this gesture which had helped him to find peace of mind.

By the time I finally visited Lindsey, towards the end of September, I had applied to another adoption agency who had immediately insisted on writing to Mr Brown to ask why I had been rejected. The reasons he had given: namely that I was cold, inflexible, mentally fragile, possessive and unable to handle rejection, were enough to put off any adoption agency, yet they were merely his subjective opinion of my personality. I was on the point of relinquishing my dream of becoming a mother but Lindsey again urged me to keep on trying and not to give up hope.

"Would you consider a boy?" she asked suddenly.

That was an easy question to answer. Although I had always longed for a daughter, the arrival of my nephew four years earlier had shown me that I could love a boy just as much. Also, part of my bias towards girls was because I had seen them as the undervalued and underprivileged sex. However true that might be in the normal world, in adoption circles it is definitely the boys who are the underdogs.

Lindsey then told me she had just heard that our local authority was looking for a home for a baby boy called Daniel with Down's Syndrome, but the only prospective adopter willing to take a Down's baby insisted that she wanted a girl. Daniel had been waiting for a family since his birth seven months earlier and his social worker Anne was anxious to find him a home as soon as possible.

As Lindsey said, this did seem like a wonderful opportunity for me but by now I was very wary of having my hopes raised again. Still the next day I contacted Anne who sounded delighted to hear from me and said that they were always looking for people to adopt babies with Down's Syndrome. After asking me a few questions, Anne arranged to come and visit me a few days later.

At our first meeting Anne told me a little about Daniel, as well as asking many searching questions about me and why I wanted to adopt. I learnt that he had been born in February and immediately taken into care, as his parents felt unable to cope with his disability. On leaving hospital he had been placed in a foster home. At first he had been very passive but was now much more alert and responsive. He was prone to chest infections and the doctors had just discovered a small hole in his heart. Knowing that half of all Down's babies have some kind of heart problem, I wasn't too alarmed by this news. Anne concluded her description with the words:

"There is something about him that makes everybody love him."

By the end of the interview, Anne seemed favourably impressed by my experience and obvious commitment and agreed to start an assessment. She did, however, warn me that

79

she was still planning to advertise for a family for Daniel in the local newspaper as she didn't want to pin all her hopes on me at this early stage.

Soon afterwards, an application form arrived from the local authority. One of the questions asked was: "Have you previously been turned down by another adoption agency?" I had no choice but to tell them about my rejection, but to my relief they decided not to contact Mr Brown, but to judge for themselves whether or not I was suitable to adopt. Once again I had to agree to a police check, have a medical examination and arrange for written references before the assessment interviews could commence.

Early in November I telephoned Anne with a query and found she had just received my medical report and was clearly worried about my psychiatric treatment fourteen years earlier. With a sinking heart I braced myself for another rejection, but instead their medical advisor seemed satisfied by my doctor's assurance that I had changed and was now a much stronger person. By the end of November, I was told that all the initial hurdles had been overcome and the interviews could now begin.

When Anne came for her second visit, I was anxious to know whether anyone else had come forward for Daniel in response to the advertisement. Anne replied that there had been some enquiries, but it was too early to say if they would come to anything. The thought of possible competition was alarming, especially as any couples coming forward were likely to be chosen in preference to me, but at least I had the advantage of being part way through the assessment.

The other news Anne brought was more encouraging. In the last couple of months two more Down's babies had come into care needing new homes, a boy and a girl. They already had someone approved for the girl, but that still left two Down's boys waiting for a family.

Anne had brought along another social worker, Janet, who would carry out my assessment as she lived nearby. Janet was around my age and I found that she was currently lecturing at my old university, which meant she could only do the interviews in the evenings, which suited me very well. We agreed that six would be a good time for us both. Just as she was leaving, Janet said:

"I'll probably be a few minutes late, as I don't want to miss the end of *Neighbours*."

"That will be fine, as long as we finish in time for *The Archers*," I replied, delighted with this human touch, in sharp contrast to the cold formality of Mr Brown, who had addressed me as Miss --------- right up to the bitter end.

Before Christmas arrived Janet managed to fit in two interviews. The first consisted of detailed questions about my life, ranging from the type of parenting I had received to details of my O and A Levels. Inevitably there were questions about my breakdown and its causes. After answering them I asked fearfully:

"Is that likely to be a major obstacle?"

"I shouldn't think so," Janet replied, looking up briefly from the notes she was frantically scribbling.

In the second interview there were a number of deep questions about my beliefs, values, lifestyle, my views on bringing up children and how I would deal with the likely problems and challenges. Several very personal questions were asked, including:

"Why have you never married?"

"How do you cope with your sexual desires?"

Janet clearly hated asking these questions far more than I minded answering them. I could see that they needed to gain a good understanding of a person's character in order to decide whether they were suitable to adopt, especially when the children available for adoption nowadays nearly always have extra problems. It sometimes seems a pity that natural parents don't have to undergo similar scrutiny before they have children. If they did, there might be fewer children in care.

After Christmas we met again in order to discuss the type of child I felt I could adopt and complete a Range of

Acceptance form. Although I was being assessed with Daniel in mind, we still had to complete the form in case that match fell through and we had to look for another child. The questions were mainly about the number of children, age range, sex and disability or family problems I could accept. Halfway down the list, which included things like epilepsy, diabetes, severe learning disability and history of abuse, one item caught my eye: red hair! I couldn't believe it. With adopters nowadays being expected to take on children with major problems, would anyone turn a child down because of their hair colour? Perhaps it was a trick question, or just a red herring?

After this interview Janet told me she was nearly ready to start her report for the adoption panel. She just needed to interview my mother and my two referees and then see me once more to tie up any loose ends. At our fourth meeting, a few weeks later, Janet assured me that she saw no reason why the panel should reject my application.

Despite this reassurance I didn't dare to raise my hopes too much. After seeing so many of my dreams die, it seemed too much to believe that this, the most outrageous and ambitious of them all, could possibly be fulfilled. Yet if it wasn't, how could I bear the crushing disappointment after coming so close to success? I had already decided that if this attempt failed, I would accept that I was meant to remain childless.

Around this time I had a very strange dream. Against all the odds, I had been allowed to adopt the child of my fantasies, a beautiful, intelligent little girl, not more than three years old, with no behaviour problems. Instead of being delighted, however, I felt nothing but coldness towards her. She was a lovely child, but she wasn't meant for me. Deep inside, I felt a longing for the little Down's boy who was out there somewhere waiting for me.

At the end of January I was sent on a one day course for prospective adopters. Although somewhat disconcerted to find myself the only single person among fourteen couples, I enjoyed the talks by social workers, an adoptive parent and an adult adoptee, as well as the discussion groups. The other prospective adopters were mostly in their thirties or forties and some had children of their own. All of them were being asked to consider adopting a school age child, or a child with special needs, or a sibling group, rather than the healthy newborn who is so rarely offered for adoption nowadays.

For me the most important piece of information came during the lunch break when I heard a couple asking one of the social workers how children were matched with adopters. She explained that normally the social workers drew up a shortlist of three prospective families and the adoption panel then chose the family they considered most suitable.

"It's different for this lady here," she said, indicating me. "She is the only one being put forward to the panel for her child."

Eagerly I questioned the social worker to ensure that I had heard correctly. Yes, it was true. I had no competition to fear. The only remaining hurdle was convincing the panel of my suitability as an adopter.

A few days later, while shopping in the supermarket, I bumped into Jean, my former Caring Group leader. She and her husband had moved to another church a few years earlier and we had lost touch. Now, as we exchanged news, I started telling her of my plans. Of all people, I was expecting Jean to be the most dubious about me adopting a child, as she had seen me at my weakest and was a cautious person by nature. For a few moments she stood silently beside the frozen vegetables taking in my news and then she said that she had seen an article about Lindsey in the local paper and had thought at the time that this was a possible answer for single women like me who longed for a child.

"I hope you are planning to have two," she added.

I assured her that if all went well with the first child, I had every intention of trying for a second one, then proceeded to the checkout, feeling greatly encouraged.

Early in February Janet visited again to show me the report she had prepared for the adoption panel, recommending my acceptance as an adopter of a Down's child under the age of two. She explained that the panel first had to approve me as an adopter and then consider separately if I was the right person for Daniel, although both these stages could be completed on the same day.

All that remained was to wait for the adoption panel to fit my application into the queue. At first Janet told me that they couldn't consider my case until 23 March, but soon afterwards it was brought forward to 8 March. Since I was already counting off the days I was delighted with this news. There was only one snag: 8 March was a Thursday!

During the final weeks of waiting, I attended a course in Makaton, a simplified sign language used to help people with learning disabilities to communicate. It is especially useful for children with Down's Syndrome who tend to find it difficult to speak clearly, partly because of their large tongues. By encouraging them to sign as well as speak, it is easier to understand what they are trying to say, reducing frustration for both themselves and their carers.

I was also very busy at work, training my successor. Usually three months notice was required for staff at my grade and above but the directors had agreed to let me give provisional notice, on the understanding that I could withdraw it if my plans fell through. They had also agreed that I could purchase my company car when I left.

At last the great day dawned. Janet had told me that the panel met in the afternoon and she would ring me at home when the meeting had finished. Returning home that evening, I took up my vigil by the telephone. After about half an hour, it finally rang.

"Are you sitting down?" Janet asked.

My heart sank, as I heard again the very words my mother had used on that other Thursday, nearly a year ago. What shock was now in store?

"Congratulations!" Janet continued. "You've got a son!"

Chapter 14

Daniel

The hours following Janet's telephone call I spent in a state of euphoria, marred only by the fear that I might wake and find it all a dream. On returning to the office the next day, I found my colleagues eagerly awaiting my news. They immediately organised a leaving collection which raised enough money to buy me the best cot in the shop. Of all the comments on my leaving card, the one that best summed up the situation was:
"Good luck in your new job. Pay: miserable; hours: long; rewards: immense."

That evening, Janet came round and I was finally able to see some photos of my new son. Unfortunately, they were too blurred to give me much idea of how he looked, although I was encouraged to see that his foster mother also wore glasses, so that would be something familiar for Daniel. I was also given some details of his birth parents – a very wealthy married couple with university degrees and successful careers – and pondered the contrast with the usual adoption scenario in which a child born to a poor single mother is given to a rich couple. It was arranged that I would visit the foster home the following week and we would then agree a series of visits to enable us to get to know each other before I brought him home.

The following Wednesday saw me knocking on the door of the foster home. A lady came to the door carrying a rather fat, unattractive looking baby in her arms.

"This must be Daniel," I said as brightly as I could, trying to conceal my disappointment.

"Oh no," she replied. "Daniel's inside."

I remembered then that she was a child minder, as well as a foster mother. As I followed her inside, I saw two more babies and this time there was no mistaking Daniel. His

85

Down's features were obvious but he had a charming little face which captivated me completely.

During the next two weeks, I made six more visits to the foster home, where I would give Daniel his lunch and play with him until he was ready for his afternoon nap. He was a happy, contented baby, who greatly enjoyed the games his foster father played with him when he returned home at lunchtime from his job as a milkman. Due to the floppy muscles which are common in Down's babies, Daniel was not yet sitting up, but he had recently learnt to roll over and was enjoying his new freedom to move around the room in this way.

In between the visits to the foster home, I fitted in my last few days at work, as well as trips to baby shops. After years of buying things for other people's babies, the thrill of shopping even for such mundane things as nappies for my own baby was immense.

Finally, the day came when I would bring Daniel back home with me for good. After putting the baby seat my sister had given me in the social worker's car, we drove off together to collect my son. Amid the excitement was the knowledge that this would be a traumatic day for the foster family, as well as a wrench for Daniel. How would he cope with being parted from the family who had loved and cared for him for over a year?

The foster parents put on a brave face and even managed to smile for the final photos, but I was not deceived. I promised them that they could come and visit Daniel in a month's time and then we said our farewells. On the return journey, Daniel slept most of the way, only waking as I carried him, still strapped in his car seat, into his new home.

The first thing Daniel did when I put him on the floor of the lounge was to roll over to the wall unit, reach up for a box of tissues and start shredding them. Immediately I put the tissues on a higher shelf, little realising that I would have to move things higher and higher over the next few months as Daniel became more mobile.

It was amazing how quickly Daniel settled into his new home. Although he had some grizzly moments, most of the time he played happily and when I put him in his new cot that first night he promptly fell asleep, never stirring until the morning. That Sunday I took him to church. So often in the past I had seen people crowd round new mothers to admire their babies. Now at last it was my turn and I loved every minute. I had already announced Daniel's expected arrival through the church newsletter and explained that I had chosen a child with Down's Syndrome, which was probably just as well. Since the date that Sunday was 1 April, if we had just turned up without prior warning people might have suspected me of playing an April fool!

My mother had come down the day before to see her new grandson and seemed delighted with him, although she later confessed that she had been dismayed by his passivity and floppiness. When I tried to help him sit up by placing him against the settee to support his back and with cushions on either side, he just flopped forward. Yet, within three weeks he was sitting unaided, which was a tremendous encouragement.

Unfortunately Daniel learnt to sit up just before the doctor came round to assess him for disability benefits. When filling in the form three weeks earlier I had stated truthfully that Daniel could not sit up, yet there he was sitting so beautifully that it looked as though I had been lying. The doctor proceeded to give such a favourable report on Daniel that my application was turned down. It took fifteen months of fighting and two appeals before the benefit was finally granted. Even then, the battle was not over, as the benefit was awarded only for three or four years at a time. At the end of each period, I would again have to complete around forty pages of forms to re-apply for the benefit. It wasn't until Daniel was fifteen years old that the benefit office finally accepted that he had a life long disability and granted him the middle rate of Disability Living Allowance for life.

My other battle at this time was with the local council. The week before bringing Daniel home, I heard that the sale of my flat had fallen through. Two days after Daniel's arrival, the infamous Poll Tax was implemented. Although this was supposed to be a tax on people rather than property, anyone with more than one property had to pay an extra 200% Poll Tax. I wrote to the council, explaining that this second property was not an asset, as it was now worth less than my bridging loan and that I was living on benefits since adopting my son with Down's Syndrome. The council were unmoved by my story, insisting that I had to pay this extra tax. Subsequent appeals through the local paper and my MP proved ineffective and things would have been desperate if my brother had not very kindly offered to pay the whole of this extra Poll Tax for as long as the council demanded it. It was a further year, during which I had to keep reducing the price, before the flat was finally sold and I was able to repay most of my mother's loan, the rest of which she agreed to cancel.

Despite these external difficulties, life with Daniel was proving much easier and far less stressful than going to work. He was such a contented baby, settling happily in his cot for his two daytime naps and sleeping well every night. His early waking, between five and six, took some getting used to, but we enjoyed our days together. Daniel shared my love of books and we spent many happy hours looking at them, while I would point to things in the pictures and name them. He also loved nursery rhymes, especially ones with actions, involving things like being bounced up and down on my lap. The only problem was that Daniel had a tendency to vomit for up to three hours after a meal or a drink, so the only really safe time to bounce him on my lap was first thing in the morning, before breakfast.

Although Daniel's vomiting was a nuisance, the way he was continuing to grow and thrive meant that it was not a major concern. During his time in the foster home, Daniel had been ill several times with chest infections, but now they were becoming far less frequent. The visits to the heart specialist also brought encouraging news as the hole in Daniel's heart proved to be very small and it was expected to close by itself (which it did by the time Daniel was six years old). Concerns remained about his hearing and we eventually discovered that he was deaf in his right ear, although strangely this has not affected his speech, which has always been remarkably clear for a Down's child.

A month after Daniel's arrival, the foster parents made their promised visit. Daniel was asleep when they arrived, but when he woke up and saw them standing round his cot, his face lit up with joy. I was pleased that he remembered them but relieved when he showed no distress at their subsequent departure. We visited the foster home a few months later and have continued to keep in touch over the years.

Before you can apply for an adoption order, the child has to live with you for at least three months, so at this stage Daniel was still officially in care and the social workers had to make regular visits. At one of these visits, they informed me that the birth mother wanted to write to me. Initially both parents had decided that they wanted no contact at all, but on receiving the letter from the social worker telling them about Daniel's placement with me, the mother had changed her mind. To my enormous relief they confirmed that she was still sure she wanted him to be adopted. In fact she had been reassured by the details they had given about me but now felt the need to stay in touch. I was more than happy to have contact provided there was no risk of the birth mother wanting Daniel back before the adoption order was made, so I told the social workers to let her go ahead.

A few weeks later the letter arrived. Daniel's birth mother, Ruth, wrote how pleased she was that he had found a home with me, that she now felt much more peaceful about the adoption and wanted to thank me for loving him. In my reply, I talked about life with Daniel and the reasons I had decided to adopt. I added that I would have found it much harder to enjoy Daniel if he had been born to me, after expecting a normal child, telling her of a couple in my church who had a profoundly disabled son around the same age as Daniel. Much as they loved him, they were still grieving terribly for the normal son they had anticipated and had now lost.

Ruth's reply showed how much she appreciated my letter and we continued to correspond around once a year until Daniel was five years old. After that, she moved (or perhaps something happened to her) and left no forwarding address for social services. To my great disappointment, I have heard nothing from her since. I still hope that she may get back in touch one day.

An extract from one of my letters to Ruth sums up my feelings at this time:

"I sometimes feel like one of the irregular shapes in Daniel's shape sorter. For years I have tried to fit into conventional shaped holes, but now I have found just the right hole for me."

Chapter 15

"Mummy"

There were plenty of visitors to our house during my first few months with Daniel. A community nurse, Pauline, came every fortnight to give advice on teaching Daniel new skills using the Portage Programme. This consists of a checklist of skills, broken down into very small steps and divided into five areas: socialisation, self-help, motor, cognitive and language. At each visit, we would decide on the tasks I would try to teach Daniel over the next two weeks. Pauline would also bring toys that were appropriate to his stage of development, like a box with a circular hole, which was later replaced by a posting box with three different shapes and holes.

Although the Portage Programme seemed like hard work at times, as a new mother I found it very helpful to have such clear guidance on the types of toys and activities that would benefit Daniel the most. Pauline would also listen to any general concerns I had over Daniel's health and other issues.

The physiotherapist and speech therapist also made regular visits. At this stage, the speech therapist was mainly concerned with moving Daniel from his bottle, which encouraged the wrong type of tongue movements, onto a trainer cup and then a normal cup. She also wanted him to progress from baby food to foods requiring more chewing since this exercise would strengthen the muscles used for speech.

Daniel was extremely reluctant to part from his bottle, so I started just using the trainer cup for one drink, most of which ended up in his bib. Gradually, over the next year, I increased the number of drinks from the trainer cup until he was only having a bottle before bedtime. Moving him away from baby food was a bigger challenge. He flatly refused to eat my food, however much I cut it up. In the end I had to mix just a tiny amount of my food in with the baby food, then gradually increase the proportion over the next few months until he finally accepted normal food.

In addition to all the contacts with various professionals, I was getting to know other mothers. Lindsey was delighted that I had succeeded in adopting at last and I found it so helpful to talk to someone in a similar position to myself, who was an expert on Down's Syndrome. Soon I made another new friend. Just before bringing Daniel home, I had made enquiries about swimming lessons for babies and when the lady asked how old Daniel was, I said:

"He's thirteen months, but he has Down's Syndrome."

"So has my little boy," she replied.

This was the start of a long friendship with Kate whose son Nathan is just a year older than Daniel. Over the years we have been able to share concerns, starting with things like how to get them feeding themselves and toilet trained when they were little, through to the question of which college they should attend and where they should live afterwards now that they are young men.

When I first brought Daniel home, several other women in the church, including my closest friend Liz, were expecting babies. For the first time I was able to share in their delight in their new babies without feeling the pang of childlessness. Liz's son was also called Daniel and it was wonderful to meet up as new mothers and talk endlessly about our babies. The church ran a mother and toddler group, as well as a women's meeting with a crèche, so there were plenty of opportunities to meet with other mothers. Pauline also started a group for mothers of children with disabilities and the local leisure centre had soft play sessions which Daniel greatly enjoyed.

In the evenings, after Daniel had gone to sleep, I would frequently go up to his room and stand over his cot, gazing at him and thinking "Isn't he lovely? Aren't I lucky?" My feelings for Daniel helped me to understand for the first time how God feels about us. For a long time I had known the Bible verse Zephaniah 3.17, which talks about God delighting in us and rejoicing over us with singing, but had never quite believed it. I didn't see how God could possibly delight in me when he knows all my imperfections, but now I was delighting in Daniel just as he was.

One of my neighbours commented on how radiant I looked as I took Daniel on outings like our regular visit to feed the ducks. Many times the thought came to my mind:
"There may be tough times ahead, but nothing can take away the wonderful time we are having now."

After Daniel had been with me for three months, I was able to apply for the adoption order and finally, a week before Christmas, we went to court. It was a very informal affair, just a meeting in a small room with the judge, the social worker, Daniel and me. The judge expressed amazement at an actuary adopting a child with a disability and said he would have to revise his former view of actuaries as heartless calculating machines. Still, he seemed satisfied that this calculating machine was capable of being a good mother and granted the adoption order.

One of the first things I did once Daniel was legally mine, was write to Mr Brown, telling him that despite his predictions I had succeeded in adopting a child and that things were going well. To his credit, he wrote a very pleasant reply, saying he was pleased that things had worked out for me and wishing me well.

I was now free to have Daniel baptised if I wished, but true to my Baptist roots, I decided to leave this until he was old enough to decide for himself and opted instead for a service of thanksgiving. The Anglican church has a special form of this service called thanksgiving after adoption. For godparents I chose the couple in my church who also had a disabled son, as well as a young man called Malcolm who had taken a great interest in Daniel. Malcolm had been a friend for some years now and was also an actuary, but there had never been any romantic interest on either side, partly because he was six years younger than me. (Once I did point out, jokingly, that actuarially speaking we were a perfect match, since we had the same life expectancy. He has since married a mutual friend, a few years younger than himself.) Having seen how well Daniel related to his foster father, it was good to see Malcolm playing with him in the same way.

The next milestone for Daniel was starting school. Already we were in the process of applying for a statement of special educational needs with a view to him starting at the nursery of the local special school the term after his second birthday. The nursery teacher warned me that the nursery was quite full, so she could only offer one morning and one afternoon a week at first. This would then increase gradually until he became a full time pupil the September after his fourth birthday.

There was at that time (and still is) a fierce debate over the relative merits of mainstream and special schools for children with Down's Syndrome. Like all mothers, I agonised over what was best for my child. In the end, the advice of all the professionals and the excellent reputation of the local special school convinced me that I should give it a try. Both Kate's son and Lindsey's two boys were also pupils at the special school, although Lindsey later moved her younger son to mainstream, so Daniel already had friends there. In the meantime, since Daniel was only a part time pupil, I would make sure that he had plenty of contact with his mainstream peers outside school.

It was quite an emotional moment seeing my baby start school before he had even learnt to walk. Still, his obvious enjoyment of school and the acceleration in his progress in all areas over the next few months confirmed that I had made the right decision.

Now I had a bit of time to myself, which was quite welcome, especially as I had started doing some tutoring for one of the correspondence courses for the actuarial examinations. While I did not miss my job at all, the tutoring provided some welcome intellectual activity. Two of my students even took the trouble to write and thank me for the helpful remarks I had made on their test papers, which was very encouraging.

By the time Daniel started school, he was twenty six months old. My friend Liz's son Daniel was sixteen months younger, but he was now catching up fast and both boys were nearly ready to walk unaided. Who would be first? I so hoped it would be my son.

Within a few days, the other Daniel took his first steps. When his father told me, his face beaming with pride: "He's walking now!" I felt like hitting him as the disparity of ability between the boys was brought home to me.

Soon afterwards, however, at twenty seven months, Daniel took four steps on his own. A few weeks later, he finally learnt to feed himself with a spoon and best of all he uttered the word I had been waiting so many years to hear: "Mummy!"

Chapter 16

Second Time Around

When Daniel was two-and-a-half, I decided the time had come to start looking for a brother or sister for him. Quite apart from my own desire for another baby, I felt that Daniel really needed a companion like himself, who would grow up with him and not overtake him in the way his mainstream friends were doing. He had certainly benefited from the close one-to-one relationship we had enjoyed in his babyhood, but in the longer term such an intense relationship could be unhealthy and stifling. Already I was aware of being overprotective towards him and had upset more than one mother by overreacting when other children hurt him. Caring for Daniel had proved easier than I had expected and I felt reasonably confident that I could manage a second child, even though I knew it would be hard work.

When I contacted social services again, they told me that I would need to repeat the assessment process, even though they had already approved me as an adopter for Daniel. Once again I was police checked, had a medical, supplied references and had a series of interviews with another social worker. This time the whole process was much less stressful and after six months the social worker wrote a glowing report for the adoption panel, which approved me for a second Down's baby. Now all I had to do was wait for a child.

By this time I had already experienced two disappointments. Shortly after the interviews had started, Daniel's former foster mother had told me that they were fostering a Down's baby girl who was due to be adopted and invited me to come and see her. After visiting them, I contacted my social worker, who informed me that social services were also assessing a couple for a Down's baby and they would almost certainly be offered this child.

The next disappointment had come two months later, when I applied for an Indian Down's baby girl advertised in the adopters' magazine. Knowing that there was a shortage of Indian adopters even for babies without any problems, I had hoped they would consider me. In my letter I stressed not only my experience with Down's babies, but the fact that my mother had grown up in India, that I had always had an interest in the country and had sponsored an Indian girl for many years, that I had worked with a number of Indian people in my last job and had Indian friends. The baby's social worker informed me that they were still hoping to find Indian parents, but if they were unsuccessful, they intended to let her white foster mother adopt her. Although deeply disappointed, I could see that it was the best solution for this little girl.

A few months after my approval as an adopter, I saw another Indian girl advertised for adoption. Although she also had Down's Syndrome, this was not obvious from her photo which reminded me strongly of my childhood friend Caroline, who had been Anglo-Burmese. (Caroline did not have Down's Syndrome.) Once again I wrote, stressing my Indian connections as well as my experience with Down's Syndrome. On receiving no reply, I telephoned the baby's social worker, who was barely civil to me once she discovered I was white. She informed me that they would only consider Indian adopters for this child, even though she had been waiting for a family for two years. Eight months later, to my fury and dismay, I saw her advertised again, still waiting for a family, yet another victim of adoption apartheid.

During this period, I also applied for three white baby girls with Down's Syndrome who were featured in the adopters' magazine, but each time I received the same reply. They had received a large response to their advertisement and I had not been included in the shortlist.

By September 1992, seven months had elapsed since my approval and I was becoming very discouraged, wondering if I would ever have a second child. Perhaps I should be content with Daniel and accept that he was to be the only one. Yet even if I could bear the disappointment for myself, I knew Daniel needed a companion. The uncertainty was an added strain. Since I had already been approved, I could have a child placed with me in a matter of weeks. On the other hand, I could go on waiting for years and never be offered a child. One evening, as I thought and prayed about it all, I made a decision. I would continue to wait for another year until Daniel started full time school. If no child arrived during that time I would assume that Daniel was meant to be the only one and start looking for a part-time job.

The following day a letter arrived, which temporarily put the whole issue out of my mind. My building society wrote to say that my mortgage payments were badly in arrears. This was alarming news as six months earlier the benefits office had taken over responsibility for paying mortgage interest for people on benefits, instead of including the money in their benefit payments. The idea of the change was to stop people on benefits from getting into arrears and losing their houses, but now I, who had never missed a mortgage payment in my life, was seriously in arrears due to a blunder by the benefits office.

Much of the morning was taken up with a series of agitated telephone calls to the building society and the benefits office as I tried to sort out this problem. Early in the afternoon, the telephone rang again. Expecting yet another call about the mortgage muddle, I wearily picked up the receiver. It was my social worker.

"We've got a baby boy for you. He's five months old and has Down's Syndrome."

A pang went through me as I said goodbye to my dream of a daughter, but this was quickly followed by excitement that the waiting was over at last and Daniel would have the brother he needed.

My social worker explained that this baby, Matthew, had been born in April and placed in foster care while his parents tried to decide whether they could look after him. After three months they had finally decided not to bring him home and had asked social services to find a couple to adopt him. The social workers had tried to follow their wishes but had been unable to find a suitable couple. Although there were plenty of couples in the county waiting to adopt, none of them wanted a child with Down's Syndrome. Eventually, after seeing the book I had prepared giving photos and details of my life and family, the parents had agreed that they were happy for me to adopt him.

Before I could meet Matthew his social worker Maureen needed to visit me and report back to the adoption panel, so that they could approve the match.

The following week, my social worker brought Maureen round to my house. While we were chatting together, Daniel wandered into the kitchen and by the time I followed him there, he had picked up the scalding hot teapot. Mercifully, I managed to take it from him before he scalded himself, but I was terrified that this momentary lapse of care on my part would count against me. Fortunately, the social workers accepted that all parents make mistakes and were happy to recommend the match to the panel, which was due to meet the following month. In the meantime I was given some photos and a short video of Matthew which showed him to be a beautiful baby.

I was told that Matthew was being fostered by a single parent who, in addition to her own son, had an adopted three year old boy with Down's Syndrome. This was the child who had been available for adoption at the same time as Daniel. When social services failed to find him a family, his foster mother had adopted him. It was good to know that Matthew was used to having a toddler brother so was less likely to be frightened of Daniel.

Three weeks later the panel finally approved the match with Matthew and the following Monday saw me making my way to his foster home. Thanks to the video, I already had some idea of what he was like, although I was dismayed to find him so overweight. In six months he had more than tripled his weight from just over five pounds at birth to eighteen pounds. Still, that would be easy to rectify over time, although it meant that I would have to forgo my dream of carrying my child in the sling I had borrowed from a friend.

Since Matthew was so young, it was decided that I would just make five visits over the next ten days and then bring him home. It was encouraging to see how tolerant Matthew was of his foster brother's rough treatment. The foster mother assured me that he was a placid easy baby and it was clear that she was very fond of him. On two of the visits I brought Daniel to see his new brother. He showed a mild interest but was more occupied with playing with the toys, little realising the significance of these visits.

Finally, at the end of October, my social worker took Daniel and me to the foster home to collect our new baby. After a tearful farewell from his foster mother, we returned home where his grandmother was awaiting his arrival. As we entered the house together I knew that at last my family was complete.

Chapter 17

Matthew

As soon as I brought Matthew into the house, Daniel went up to him and pulled off his socks. He soon became fascinated by the small person who had invaded his life, treating him rather like a new toy. I never received the impression that he resented the newcomer but like most toddlers he could be very rough with him, trying to push him over or even tread on him. Clearly I could never risk leaving them alone together, even for a minute.

My mother was quite dismayed by Daniel's treatment of Matthew, saying that he was as rough as my brother had been with my sister as a baby. By contrast, my nephew had been positively angelic towards his baby sister, adoring her from the very start. Still, whilst Daniel's behaviour might be undesirable, it seemed much more normal to me. At least Matthew was not a vulnerable newborn but a sturdy lad of six months who had become used to rough toddlers.

One advantage of Daniel's treatment of Matthew was that I became much more relaxed when other children hurt Matthew at toddler group. Instead of becoming upset and making a fuss, I would say to the apologetic mother: "Don't worry. He's used to much worse from his brother."

Fortunately, Matthew was generally a placid, happy baby, who showed no fear of his brother and seemed to enjoy his company. At bedtime, however, he became a different child.

On that first night, as soon as I put Matthew in his cot, he started screaming and nothing seemed to pacify him. I tried rocking him to sleep in my arms, but as soon as I put him down he woke up and the screaming started again. Next, I tried leaving him in the cot and checking him at regular intervals, but the screaming persisted for over an hour before he eventually wore himself out and fell asleep.

Little did I know then that this pattern would be repeated many times over the coming months. After Daniel, who had always settled happily in his cot, playing with his toys until he fell asleep, this was such a shock. There were times over the next few months that I ended up going into my room and punching a pillow to relieve my frustration and for the first time I understood why some parents batter their children when they won't stop crying.

There was no question of Matthew settling in his cot for his daytime naps, so instead he would just fall asleep whenever he felt like it, frequently at the most inconvenient times, like in the middle of his tea. After such a late nap, he would not be ready for bed until late evening. Instead of the fixed routine I had been able to establish with Daniel, life was now much more unpredictable.

It was certainly exhausting coping with two small children but at least Daniel was now attending nursery for three days a week. I sometimes wondered how mothers cope when they have two little ones at home all the time. Like many mothers, I felt guilty that I was unable to give my second child the attention that his brother had known. I sometimes consoled myself with the thought that, since his birth parents had other children, he would have been in a similar position if he had remained with them. Matthew's birth parents had declined the opportunity to meet me, but I had been given some information about them, their families and their medical history. They asked me to send them an annual letter, which I have done ever since, but they have never felt able to reply.

When Matthew first arrived, I was attending a support group for prospective and new adopters. At one meeting, around three months after Matthew's arrival, one of the adopters, Sue, was distraught because the baby that had been placed with her a few weeks earlier had just been taken away, after the birth mother changed her mind. Sue and her husband had been overjoyed to be offered a healthy baby, after being told to expect an older child, but now their dreams were shattered. Amid my concern for her grief was the thought:

"What if this happened to me?" Although it seemed unlikely that Matthew's birth parents would change their minds after all this time, I grew increasingly impatient for the adoption order, which was finally granted six months after I brought Matthew home.

About a year later, I met Sue in the supermarket and found that she had just been offered a toddler. Since this child was the subject of a Care Order, the parents could not take her back, so the adoptive parents were spared the fear of the same thing happening again. Although no-one could replace the child they had lost, it was good to know that they had been given a second chance of parenthood.

Appearing in public with two Down's children inevitably attracted a good deal of attention, most of which was positive. In any case, my lack of awareness of people's reactions meant that I remained oblivious to all but the most blatant stares. On outings with my friend Kate and her Down's son, she has often noticed and commented on people's reactions to the boys, which have totally passed me by. One day, however, my family encountered an attitude that even I could not ignore.

On a visit to the doctor, I walked into the waiting room, where a woman looked up and said:

"It's obvious they are not yours. No-one could be that unlucky!"

For a moment I was speechless. There were so many things I could have said to this ignorant and insensitive woman but I was too stunned to think of them. Instead, I merely replied:

"Actually they are mine, by adoption."

I went on to tell her that I knew of more than one family who had two Down's children born to them. (I was afraid she might repeat her crass remark to one of them, causing further distress to those who had already been through enough grief.)

Undaunted, she then remarked that my younger one didn't seem too bad, unlike his brother, perhaps assuming that as a mere adoptive parent I had no feelings.

I encountered a similar attitude from an old lady to whom I gave lifts to the meeting for retired people at the church. On looking at Matthew she said:

"He's not too badly disfigured."

"Neither are you," I felt like saying, but instead I replied:

"I think he's beautiful."

The mother of one of Matthew's classmates once described him as drop dead gorgeous, so I know it isn't just a mother's bias that causes me to think that he is a very good looking boy.

Meanwhile the Community nurse was still visiting and somehow we managed to find time for the Portage games and exercises. Matthew was responding well and actually sat up unaided by the time he was ten months old. He was less floppy than Daniel had been and far less inclined to vomit after feeds, which came as a relief. Generally he seemed remarkably healthy with no heart problem or any concerns over his sight or hearing.

With Matthew doing so well, I was fully expecting another fight when claiming disability benefits and sure enough, we were turned down. This time, thanks to my experience of such things, it only took one appeal before the decision was reversed and he was granted the middle rate of Disability Living Allowance up to the age of five.

The knowledge I had gained with Daniel made me much more confident with Matthew, despite the differences between them. Like Daniel, he was very reluctant to move from baby food to my meals and for a long time he refused to try any finger foods but I knew we would get there eventually. Matthew was less fond of books than his brother, preferring more active pursuits, but he shared Daniel's love of action rhymes.

Once Matthew was sitting up, I was able to bath them together and they enjoyed this time immensely, especially when I ducked down beside the bath and then reappeared saying: "Peepbo!" The first time I would say it softly, then a little louder and the third time I would shout it out, accompanied by shrieks of delight from them both. As time went on the boys were able to play together more and more and their enjoyment of each other confirmed that despite the hard work, two was better than one. Nevertheless, it was a relief when Daniel started school full time, in the autumn of 1993. Soon afterwards, we started applying for Matthew's statement of special educational needs so that he could start nursery for two mornings a week the following April. After the hectic months following Matthew's arrival, life was beginning to settle down again. The school holidays were always a challenge but my mother made frequent visits to help out for a few days and Daniel was now old enough to attend the special needs playscheme held for a week each summer and a couple of days at Easter. In the summer of 1994, we even managed to go away on holiday. It was hard work, but thanks to my mother's help I was able to cope and even enjoy the break.

Chapter 18

Pride Comes Before a Fall

Shortly before Matthew's second birthday, I decided to move to a new church. Since the arrival of the new vicar, a few years earlier, quite a number of people had left the church, some moving to another Anglican church and others to the local Baptist, while many who remained were dissatisfied. Although the new vicar did his best, he lacked the preaching gift of his predecessor and seemed to distrust any display of emotion. The services had become for me nearly as dry and boring as those of my childhood and once again I found myself factorising the hymn numbers to pass the time during sermons. In addition, I had strongly disagreed with the vicar's refusal to allow the mother of my godchildren to remarry in church. Unlike the previous vicar, who had been prepared to consider each case on its merits, this vicar had a blanket ban on the remarriage of divorcees. I had no hesitation in pointing out how cruel and unfair I believed his decision to be, for two people who had already been through the anguish of being deserted by their spouses for someone else. Although I had disagreed with the previous vicar on a number of occasions, there was always a mutual respect and willingness to acknowledge the other's good qualities, which was totally lacking with his successor.

 The fact that most of my friends were still at the church had made me reluctant to leave and make a new start elsewhere, until a clash with the vicar's wife convinced me that it was impossible to stay. Like her husband, she viewed my habit of saying exactly what I thought with alarm and after one women's meeting, during which I had been particularly outspoken, she told me I would not be allowed to attend unless I changed. Realizing that to continue at a church where I felt so negative about the leaders would only lead to further conflict, which would be bad for everyone, I decided to try the Baptist church. The year before adopting Daniel I had joined some of the people from this church on a trip to Israel and had been very impressed by their minister, so it seemed the obvious choice.

My first few weeks at the Baptist church confirmed that this was the right move. Both the boys were welcomed into the children's groups and the leader of Daniel's group immediately arranged for him to have a one-to-one helper, which was needed because of his tendency to eat crayons, glue and playdoh, as well as running off when given the chance. Matthew didn't need a helper at that stage since the crèche workers found him fairly easy to manage, although it was a different story when he was in the church with me for the first part of the service. Some years earlier, the pews at the Baptist church had been removed and replaced with comfortable chairs. The only drawback was that Matthew, who had just started to crawl, would disappear under the chairs and re-emerge several rows in front, whereas at least in the pews at the old church I had been able to stop him escaping. Still, no-one seemed to mind his antics.

The services at the new church were so lively that they reminded me of Spring Harvest, the big Christian festival that I had attended a few times with a group from my old church, despite the vicar's disapproval. Instead of the dry lectures to which I had become accustomed, the sermons were full of practical advice on how to apply what was in the Bible to your everyday life. Like someone emerging from semi-starvation to a place of plenty, I couldn't get enough of the sermons and started to order tapes of the evening services so that I could listen to them at home. Certainly there was no danger here that I would want to pass the time factorising hymn numbers, which was just as well, since the hymn books had been replaced by an overhead projector showing the worship songs and hymns on a screen.

I found several people whom I knew already at my new church and was getting to know others through their mother and toddler group. Within a month of joining the church I started asking to become a full member. In Baptist churches there are no bishops and each church is run by the members, who elect the leaders. Any major decisions have to be passed by the members at the regular members' meetings. I had been a member of my parents' church for several years, before moving to an Anglican church, which did not have an official membership, so was confident that this would be a formality.

When the assistant minister came to interview me about membership, he questioned me closely about my reasons for leaving my previous church. He said it was too soon to consider becoming a member in case I suddenly decided I didn't like this church either and went elsewhere. I pointed out that I had stayed fifteen years at my previous church, but he still said I must wait six months and then they would get a report on me from my vicar. Knowing that the vicar was unlikely to give a favourable report on someone who had clashed with both him and his wife this was not good news, but I had no option but to wait in patience.

By the end of the six months waiting period, I was more certain than ever that this was the right place for me. I had now joined a house group with very caring and supportive leaders. Also, after I had damaged one of the wheels of my car by scraping against a wall in the church car park one Sunday, I had received a telephone call from one of the ministers, saying that someone who wished to remain anonymous had offered to help pay for any repairs. Although I had declined the offer, since I had savings that would more than cover the cost, the fact that someone had cared enough to make it meant a great deal.

Early in November 1994, I was summoned to a meeting of the two ministers and the church elder to hear my fate. They said that although I was more than welcome to attend the church and the various groups they held during the week, I could not become a full member because I had upset several people at my last church and clashed with those in authority.

Although I was no stranger to rejection, this was by far the most humiliating I had ever known. After years of people telling me what a wonderful person I was to adopt my children, suddenly I was not considered good enough to join one of the least exclusive clubs in existence. It was virtually unheard of for anyone who had been baptised in one Baptist church to be refused membership of another, unless they were deliberately persisting in some gross sin. Over the past few months I had seen several people welcomed into membership, mostly new Christians from all kinds of backgrounds. At my previous church I had led many Bible studies and even the vicar's wife had acknowledged my gift for Bible teaching, yet now I was being asked to take a lower place than these new members.

Even worse than the humiliation, was the feeling of being unwanted. During my entire adult life the Christian community had been the one place where I was guaranteed acceptance, no matter how much rejection I received from outside, so this felt like the ultimate rejection. (I know that the leaders didn't intend it as a rejection, but as a form of discipline, designed to help, but that isn't how it felt at the time.)

Looking back, I think that the leaders, in their ignorance of my Aspergers, may have judged me too harshly. My inability to hide my faults and tendency to say exactly what I think makes me seem worse than others who are more skilful at hiding their darker side. Also, I read recently that people with Aspergers can seem to be deliberately challenging authority when in fact they are expressing anxiety or acting in ignorance of the social rules. There are also times when it is right to challenge those in leadership when they are acting unjustly or ignoring the needs of those who cannot fight for themselves, but it is hard for people with Aspergers to do this tactfully without causing unnecessary offence.

The Asperger obsession with getting the facts right can also lead to problems. My habit of going up to preachers after the service and pointing out mistakes in their sermons was probably seen merely as a desire to undermine their authority and show off my extensive Bible knowledge. Whilst not entirely innocent of either of these charges, my chief motivation was my obsession with factual accuracy. As a small child I had once told the little boy next door a Bible story. Afterwards, my sister informed me that I had got one of the facts wrong. Immediately I felt terribly guilty, thinking that I had told this boy a lie.

Another thing that people with Aspergers can find very upsetting is when a church service goes on after it is supposed to finish, usually because the sermon is too long. If the person remonstrates with the preacher afterwards, or even walks out before the end, this can seem like deliberate and unnecessary rudeness to those who are unaware how distressing it is for us when people do not obey the rules.

Nevertheless, no matter how badly I may have been misunderstood, there is no denying that the praise I had received since adopting the children had gone to my head. I had become arrogant and careless of people's feelings and needed to have my pride broken in order to emerge as a nicer, more likeable person.

One of the criticisms that had been made of me was my obsession with fairness. I now realise that this is part of the Asperger passion for justice, which can be a positive quality when it spurs people to help the disadvantaged and fight for the oppressed, but is deeply destructive when the slightest hint of unfair treatment leads to resentment and bitterness. At the time, all I knew was that for my own peace of mind I had to let go of this obsession with being treated fairly and save my passion for justice for championing those who were suffering much more flagrant forms of unfairness. In any case, whether my present treatment was fair or not, my reaction as a Christian should be the same: to accept the humiliation without bitterness, forgive those who inflicted it and try to learn from the experience.

One thing was clear: if I couldn't cure myself of saying exactly what I thought, then I would need to work hard to ensure that my thoughts were acceptable. This is no bad discipline for a Christian as the Bible makes it clear that God isn't interested in outward appearance but in the state of our hearts.

Staying at that church after this humiliation was one of the hardest things I have ever had to face, but I knew it was where I was meant to be. This was confirmed two weeks later when the church held a series of special meetings one weekend. Having found a friend to babysit, I was able to attend two of the meetings during which a number of us received prayer and were filled with the Holy Spirit in a way I hadn't witnessed since leaving university. As I was prayed for, another layer of bitterness fell away and I was able to forgive a number of people, including God, who I had secretly resented all my life for not allowing me to die on the day I was born and escape a world full of suffering.

The leaders noticed the change in me and six months later they agreed to recommend my acceptance for membership at the next members' meeting where it was passed unanimously. Interestingly, the period from rejection to acceptance – exactly twenty seven weeks - was identical to the interval between my rejection and subsequent acceptance as an adopter. What was more, once again both events happened on a Thursday!

Later that year, Andrew Davies' famous adaptation of *Pride and Prejudice* appeared on television. As I relived the story, I identified strongly with Darcy, who like me had become arrogant and had his pride broken by a totally unexpected and humiliating rejection. His complete honesty and integrity, combined with his love for Elizabeth, made him choose to acknowledge his faults and strive to overcome them instead of reacting with bitterness and a desire for revenge. I also understood for the first time that when something is withheld that you thought was yours for the asking, the desire for it becomes much stronger. Previously I had thought, as Elizabeth herself had done, that the scruples which had kept Darcy from proposing for so long, should have effectively quenched any desire to marry her after his devastating rejection.

As I videotaped each episode of *Pride and Prejudice* and watched it again and again, I noticed for the first time that it was possible to tell what Darcy was thinking, just by looking at his face. Of course, I was helped by two things: my knowledge of the book and the fact that I could look at Darcy's face without any risk of eye contact. In real life, it is much less easy to read a face, but now I knew that it was possible. Even if I still found it hard to read other people's faces, I now realised that they could read mine, which was in some ways quite an alarming thought. Perhaps that is why I am often more comfortable talking to friends on the telephone than speaking face to face.

Chapter 19

Back to Work

By the autumn of 1995, Matthew was spending three days a week at the special nursery, as well as one morning at the church pre-school. For the first time since adopting my second child, I felt I had some time on my hands. Knowing that in another year he would be at school full time, I thought that the following September would be a good time to return to work, if a suitable job could be found.

Realistically, I knew that with the demands of my family, I could work a maximum of three days a week, within school hours and would be able to do very little work if any in school holidays. It was now nearly six years since I had last worked as an actuary or touched a computer and I was approaching forty. What were my chances of finding a suitable job? Pretty slim, I decided. In any case, there was no point in looking until much nearer the time.

In the meantime, my mother asked me to consult a financial advisor to see if she could invest some money to pay for the care I might need in my old age. Whilst the benefits I received were adequate for my present needs, we were both aware that I had little pension provision and I was unable to save for the future without my benefits being cut. I certainly had no wish to end up like Lindsey's uncle, who after bringing up his twelve foster children single handed and saving the State a fortune, finished his days in dire poverty.

The financial advisor was required under the "know your customer" rules, to ask all kinds of questions about my financial situation. On hearing that I was an actuary, he said that he knew an actuary who was desperate for a part-time assistant. He had recently been diagnosed with a slow growing but incurable form of cancer and he was about to lose his current assistant who was seventy and wanted to retire completely. His office was less than three miles from my home and the work was in pensions, which had been my speciality.

My first reaction was: "It's too soon. I'm not ready to go back yet," but the financial advisor persuaded me to give the actuary a ring and he invited me round for an interview.

When I met Brian, the actuary, I explained my situation, saying that I would only be able to do two mornings a week until September, after which I could work for up to three days a week but would need extra time off in school holidays. After thinking it over, he agreed to give me a trial, starting in January.

During my first week at work, while looking through a file to find the data I needed for my calculations, I discovered some very angry letters my boss had written. Whilst allowing for the strain he must be under, after being diagnosed with a terminal illness, I wondered if I could work for someone who expressed himself so aggressively. His secretary, Brenda, was a friendly, approachable lady, so I confided in her that I had seen these letters and had been surprised by their tone. She told me that Brian could be very blunt in his manner and would tell people exactly what he thought of them, but on the positive side, he was incapable of telling a lie. Beneath the blunt, sometimes rude exterior, was a decent and caring man.

I had already experienced Brian's complete honesty. At the interview, instead of trying to sell me the job, he had confessed that I might find the work boring, as parts of it were quite repetitive. (Little did he realise how well this would suit me, due to my Aspergers.) He had also explained that he did all his calculations manually. Whilst this would have put off many people, for me that was another advantage. I had not worked with computers for long enough to be comfortable with them and often felt they spoiled the fun of doing calculations by hand.

During the interview I had been just as unguarded. When Brian told me how much he had paid his previous assistant, I blurted out: "That's generous!" Of course, it would have been much wiser to keep silent, or even feign a look of disappointment.

Another thing that had struck me was Brian's comment when he said he wanted to give me a very short notice period. He had said:

"It would be very awkward for us to go on sharing an office if we found we couldn't stand each other."

Brenda also warned me that Brian became very annoyed if he felt people were taking advantage of him, even in a minor way. There had been trouble with the previous tenants of the upstairs offices because Brian had complained about trivial things, like their fridge using too much electricity. Yet he was no miser, she told me. He and his wife supported charities and sponsored more than one child in poor countries.

I could understand Brian's attitude. It was not meanness but an obsessive need for fairness and to be in control that I recognised. Shortly before adopting Daniel, I had accompanied my sister and her family on a self-catering holiday. During that week I had become upset because my brother-in-law was not doing his fair share of the washing up and wanted us to draw up a rota but my sister wouldn't hear of it. She had also become irritated by my need to know each evening what we were going to do the next day, preferring to decide things on the spur of the moment.

Although I still knew nothing of Aspergers, I could see in Brian many of my own traits and wondered how I would get on with someone who seemed to be an exaggerated version of myself. Brian later told me that one of the reasons he had started his own business was because he found it so difficult working with colleagues, some of whom he couldn't stand. On another occasion he mentioned how hurt he had been by a comment someone made at his previous church, implying that he was all brain with no heart. As my father and I had found, people failed to realise that despite the abrasive manner, this was a sensitive person who was easily hurt.

Whilst the similarities between Brian and me did produce minor clashes at times, they also helped us to understand each other and we established a good working relationship. Of course it was in both our interests to get on together as he would not easily have found another qualified actuary willing to work part-time and without a computer. I would probably have found it even harder to find another job that suited me so well.

As well as necessity, the mutual respect between us enabled Brian and me to work well together. I admired his integrity, his devotion to his family (although I am sure he was not an easy person to live with) and his kindness to Jim, a man with mental health problems, who frequently visited the office. Although Brian detested the smell of smoke which always hung about Jim, he would listen to Jim pouring out his troubles and would periodically give him small amounts of money to help him out.

Perhaps more than anything I admired Brian's courageous attitude to his illness. Each afternoon I would see him in obvious pain after his lunch, but he made light of it and never complained. Despite his failing strength, he would sometimes take his older son on sailing trips at the weekend, to give him good times to remember him by. When the deterioration in his health finally forced him to sell the business, four years after I started work, he went on working from his hospital bed right up to the week before he died in order to complete the paperwork for his successor. Brian and his wife were members of a local Anglican church and they clearly had a real faith that helped them through their ordeal.

Brian in turn admired me for adopting my boys and he was always very understanding if I needed time off at short notice due to illness or a family crisis. We agreed that I would work for just one or two mornings a week during school holidays and social services paid for a sitter to come and look after the boys while I was at work.

The office was in a small house with just two rooms and a storeroom downstairs, a single toilet at the top of the stairs, with rooms on either side and a kitchen round the corner. The two rooms on the first floor were let to another company and the people always kept their doors open so that they could communicate with each other. This meant that anyone entering or leaving the toilet did so in full view of the people in the offices. At one time, this would have made the job impossible for me but thanks to the cognitive behaviour therapy all those years ago, it was no more than a minor embarrassment (or should I say an inconvenience?).

It was not just the hours and location that made this job ideal for me. With no team to manage and no client meetings, I was able to concentrate solely on the technical side of the job, which was what I did best. Life was now very busy, but the contrast between my responsibilities at home and at work made each a delightful break from the other. For the first time ever, I felt fulfilled both intellectually and emotionally and life was good.

Chapter 20

Delights and Difficulties

While I was enjoying my return to the workplace, the boys were making good progress at their special school. They also had the opportunity to attend a mainstream school for one afternoon a week, with a one-to-one helper.

Daniel's speech was improving all the time and when the school started him on the Oxford Reading Tree at the age of seven, he progressed through the books at a pace that would have put many a mainstream child to shame. Doubtless his great love of books spurred him on. I had always hoped for a child who shared my passion for books and was delighted when he started reading them himself.

Matthew was slower in his speech than Daniel and I had to wait until he was four years old before he said: "Mummy." Until then, when I collected him from nursery or crèche, he would greet me with the word: "Dinner!" showing where his priorities lay. Whereas Daniel's first word had been: "No!" Matthew's was "More!" and his first phrase was: "More dinner!"

When Daniel had been younger, I used to give him his dinner, saying warningly: "It's hot!" It was only when he started demanding: "More hot!" that I realised I had misled him into thinking that was the name for his food.

Despite taking longer to learn to speak and later to read, Matthew proved to be much quicker than Daniel in learning self-help skills. After spending two years teaching Daniel how to put on his socks, I was dreading having to go through it again with Matthew, but he learnt without being taught, simply by observing his brother. More recently, he mastered the art of tying shoelaces in three days, which was much quicker than I managed to learn it as a child. Daniel did eventually learn how to tie his shoelaces in his early teens but it took many months of effort.

As the boys increased in understanding, we were able to play many games together. We particularly enjoyed acting out stories in books. With the help of a play tunnel and play house, we would do the story of *Winnie The Pooh* getting stuck in the rabbit hole and having to be pulled out. Another favourite story was *Tigger gets Unbounced*. True to their personalities, Daniel would play Pooh and Matthew would be Tigger, while I played Rabbit. Matthew particularly enjoyed the end of the story, when as a repentant Rabbit I would greet him rapturously, throwing my arms round him and exclaiming how glad I was to see him.

The boys also loved going on outings, particularly anywhere with animals, like a farm or a zoo, or just the nearby duck pond. When they were small, I would push Matthew in the buggy and have Daniel on reins, but now they were getting older, even the reins were becoming inappropriate. As a result, I sometimes ended up losing one of them for a few minutes since one would run off while I was watching the other. I would then have to say to people:

"Have you seen a little boy with Down's Syndrome? Like him, but bigger" (or "Like him, but smaller" depending on which one I had lost.)

People have frequently remarked on the similarity in appearance of my two boys, which is not solely due to sharing the same syndrome. Their eyes and hair are the same colour and their general resemblance makes many astonished to learn that they are not related by blood. To me, it just shows that they were meant to be brothers.

The relationship between the boys at this stage was very strong. When one was upset, the other would comfort him and Daniel would often spring to Matthew's defence when I was getting cross with him. When Matthew was flatly refusing to obey me, Daniel would intervene and somehow manage to persuade him to co-operate. Although it sometimes felt as though they were ganging up on me, I was delighted to see them getting on so well.

When Daniel was seven years old, I decided the time had come to explain about his adoption and Down's Syndrome. Both boys had come to me with life story books, containing their baby photos as well as pictures of their birth and foster parents and briefly describing their life before adoption. From their earliest years I had used these books to explain to each in turn that he had grown in A's tummy, but she and her husband B had not been able to look after him, which made them very sad. He had lived with Aunty C (and Uncle D in Daniel's case) while another lady E looked for a new mummy. She had chosen me, which made me very happy and I had brought him home.

Now I decided to retell the story from my point of view, introducing the fact that they had Down's Syndrome. I said that once upon a time I had lived all alone and was very sad because I wanted a baby and couldn't grow one in my tummy because there was no daddy. Then someone told me that a lady called E could help me, so I had telephoned her, saying:

"I want to adopt a baby with Down's Syndrome."

"Well, I know a baby with Down's Syndrome who needs a new mummy," she replied. "He's called Daniel."

I explained how I had then had to wait several months while E got to know me and made sure I was good enough to be his mummy, then at last I was able to bring him home. I described how he had learnt to sit up, crawl, walk and talk and how I had then gone back to E, saying that I wanted another baby with Down's Syndrome. After a long wait, I had been told they had a second baby for me, so I took him home and called him Matthew.

It was hard to tell how much Daniel understood, but he loved the story and asked for it several times a week. As I hoped, he happily accepted Down's Syndrome as part of his identity. The only drawback was that he would often ask in a loud voice if someone he saw in the street had Down's Syndrome. The most embarrassing moment was when he went up to a Chinese couple and said:

"Has your baby got Down's Syndrome?"

(I don't think she had, but Daniel was misled by her oriental features.)

Living with my boys, I was no stranger to embarrassing incidents. In some ways, my memories of my own social blunders made it easier for me to cope with theirs. At least they had the advantage of an obvious disability that made people excuse their behaviour to some extent. Nevertheless, there was one incident at church when Daniel was nine which left me completely mortified.

Daniel loved church and would always go to the front and dance during the songs. No-one minded, in fact many people felt he was an example to the rest of us in his obvious enjoyment of the service. One Sunday, however, he started to get a bit silly, encouraged by some sniggering boys in the front row. Deciding to give them something worth laughing about, he suddenly pulled down his trousers and pants. To make matters worse, we were without a minister at that time and had invited a prospective minister to come and preach a trial sermon. This is known in Baptist circles as "Preaching with a view." As someone commented afterwards, he certainly had a view!

Afterwards I felt so ashamed I wondered how I could face people in church again, even though no-one had complained. That evening, however, when praying about it, I felt that God was saying:

"Do you think I was offended by Daniel's behaviour today? I'm far more offended by those who behave beautifully in church on the outside, but are secretly harbouring hateful thoughts"

This was some comfort to me. We never saw that minister again, but I was told that this was for reasons unconnected with Daniel.

Generally it was Matthew's behaviour that was causing me greater concern. Just before his fifth birthday, I was rushed to hospital with appendicitis. My mother came over to care for the boys and the church organised a rota of people to come and help each day. During this time, Matthew started trying to get his grandmother's attention by touching her bottom. She became very angry and smacked him hard. Instead of being deterred, he was delighted by the reaction he had provoked and did it all the more. This habit of touching bottoms has continued into his teenage years, despite all the efforts of his schools and behaviour strategies at home. He also loves touching faces, something he knows I particularly hate, however hard I try not to show it.

Unlike his brother, Matthew finds it hard to sit still and passively watch something and this has made him very difficult to manage in church, or on outings to the cinema or a live performance. At home, he would not want to watch a video for more than a very short time and if I tried to watch television, read a book or talk to a friend, he would immediately do all he could to get my full attention.

Toilet training was another source of tension. Daniel had taken a long time before he was dry during the day, but by the age of six he was fairly reliable both by day and night. The summer after he turned six, Matthew was also dry at night, but was still having frequent accidents during the day. What was worse, I strongly suspected that some of these "accidents" were deliberate attention seeking devices.

As soon as Matthew got into bed, he would wet himself, even though he had just been to the toilet and would be dry throughout the night. The first time he did this, I was about to go out and the babysitter had just arrived. Clearly, it was a form of protest. Soon this became a nightly occurrence, until I put a small pad in his pants, which would then remain dry until the morning. Whenever we went anywhere, he would invariably wet himself the moment we arrived. Remembering my own experiences, I had always vowed I would never get cross with a child for wetting themselves or asking for the toilet, but it was impossible not to feel angry when I was so sure it was deliberate.

Mixed with the frustration and anger was a terrible guilt that I was unable to love my younger son as much as his brother. As a child, sensing my parents' preference for my sister I had declared that I would love my children equally, yet however hard I tried, I had never been able to love him as well as Daniel. Did he sense this and was that why he was so difficult? He did not appear to be an unhappy child, however, just one who derived great pleasure from winding people up. Perhaps one day someone will discover a new condition called APD (Annoying People Disorder), which will explain Matthew's behaviour.

There were times during that autumn of 1998 (and in more recent years) that I was tempted to wish I had stopped at one child, yet the continuing bond between the brothers made me glad for their sakes that they had each other. Then, just as I thought life could not get any more difficult, Matthew became ill.

Early in December, Matthew started wetting the bed. Although this was disappointing, I assumed that it was just a temporary setback, probably due to the cold weather. Over the next two weeks, however, he seemed to be visiting the toilet more and more often and demanding frequent drinks. His tiredness and lack of interest in his food was an additional worry. In the middle of all this, the central heating broke down. Since this happened just before the weekend, it took a few days to get it fixed, temporarily distracting me from Matthew's problems.

The school were also becoming concerned over Matthew and suggested I should take him to the doctor. To my enormous relief, he diagnosed a simple throat infection and prescribed antibiotics. Persuading Matthew to take the medicine was no easy task, but with the aid of a pipette I managed to get it into his mouth and he soon learnt that if he spat it out he would only be given more.

During the next four days, despite the medicine, Matthew's condition was worse than ever. His thirst was now insatiable and even after he had been given four drinks in under an hour, he was still crying pitifully for more. One evening, three days before Christmas, as I was bathing him and trying to stop him drinking the bath water, I noticed that he had become thinner.

Suddenly, I remembered a story I had read in a woman's magazine thirty years earlier about a little girl called Julie. Like Matthew, she had developed an insatiable thirst, made frequent trips to the toilet and had lost weight. I then knew what was wrong with my son: diabetes.

Chapter 21

Another Disability

That night, sleep eluded me as I tossed and turned, contemplating life with a diabetic child. I just could not cope, I decided, clinging desperately to the hope that I might have been mistaken. The next morning saw me returning to the doctor's surgery, waving a urine sample and demanding that he tested it for diabetes.

Within a couple of minutes the doctor turned to me, confirming my worst fears. Immediately he telephoned the hospital, arranging for Matthew to be admitted that day. In the meantime, I had to find someone to care for Daniel. My mother was due to come over the following day for the Christmas holiday but was unable to travel any sooner. Fortunately, a new respite centre for children with special needs had opened earlier that year. My boys had already visited during the day and were due to spend two nights a month there from the beginning of January. The staff at the centre agreed to take Daniel straight away as an emergency placement, enabling me to stay with Matthew at the hospital.

Still in a state of shock, I could hardly get my mind to focus on the things we would need to pack for our overnight stays. Eventually we were ready and after dropping Daniel at the respite centre, Matthew and I made our way to the Accident and Emergency Department, where we prepared ourselves for the inevitable two hour wait.

I was no stranger to this part of the hospital, having waited there on several other occasions when Daniel had fallen and hurt himself or eaten something inedible, like a plastic coin or dog dirt. This was the first time that Matthew had been the cause of the emergency as he was far less accident prone.

At last, we found ourselves on the children's ward, where a specialist diabetes nurse told me that Matthew's condition was caused by his immune system attacking the insulin producing cells in his pancreas. The insulin was needed to convert the sugar in his blood to energy and the lack of insulin had caused his blood sugar to rise to dangerous levels. His body had tried to get rid of the excess sugar in his urine which was why he had been going to the toilet so often and had then needed to drink more, as he became dehydrated. In order to get the energy it needed, his body had started to break down fat, leading to weight loss. In the process of breaking down the fat, the body had released poisonous ketones, which would eventually have led to a coma, if we had not discovered the diabetes in time.

The nurse started to explain about the two insulin injections and blood tests Matthew would need each day. She told me that I would need to record all the insulin doses and blood test results in a book, which I would then use to work out whether the amount of insulin needed to be changed.

I was also told that Matthew would need a low sugar diet and sugar free drinks to help keep his blood sugars stable and I would need to ensure that the amount of food he ate was just sufficient to match his insulin dose. If he had too much food, his blood sugar would go too high, "a hyper" and if there was insufficient it would go too low, "a hypo". Both these conditions were dangerous, so it would be a constant balancing act to ensure that his food and insulin dose were properly matched.

As I struggled to take in all this information, my first thought was:

"I can't possibly manage all that. I was only just coping before this happened."

Then I realised that I had no choice. After six years of caring for Matthew, there was no way I could abandon him, yet this new burden was too much.

As I forced myself to read the booklets the diabetes nurse had given me, I compared it with the state of happy anticipation in which I had read the books on Down's Syndrome. Now here was a condition I had not chosen and in which I had no interest. For the first time, I really knew how it felt to be the mother of a disabled child.

That evening, Matthew had his first insulin injection. Throughout the night, nurses would come at regular intervals to do a blood test, waking both of us in the process. By the morning, however, there was good news. Matthew's blood sugar was down to near normal levels and his nappy was dry.

During his illness, Matthew had lost all bladder control and was now back in nappies day and night. After four years of toilet training, I felt we had gone back to square one, but that was the least of my worries.

That day, which was Christmas Eve, the nurses tried to teach me how to do blood tests and injections. One of the nurses let me practise my injection technique on her, but I was nowhere near ready to do them myself without supervision. On the other hand, I was desperate to return home that evening, so that I could fill the boys' stockings and we could spend Christmas Day together. Finally, it was agreed that we could go home after tea, provided we came back to the hospital for the breakfast and teatime injections.

The Christmas stockings seemed very meagre once I had taken out the sweets and chocolate, but at least we were home. The only problem was that there were no sugar free drinks or low sugar puddings in the house and the shops were now closed for the Christmas break.

Matthew's illness had made him unusually docile. Although this made it much easier for me to learn how to do his blood tests and injections, it was desperately sad to see my little Tigger without his bounce. As he recovered over the next few days, like Rabbit in the story *Tigger gets Unbounced*, I welcomed back the Tigger whose bounces were such a special part of his personality.

At first, it was the blood tests I found hardest. Being squeamish anyway, the act of squeezing a large drop of blood from Matthew's finger was almost as bad for me as it was for him. Nowadays we have a meter that requires only a tiny drop of blood, but the meters available then needed much more, which meant that it would sometimes take several attempts. Then Matthew started resisting the injections, struggling and running away. At one point, the only way I could do them was by wrestling him to the floor and sitting on him, which felt so brutal. Daniel would cry and say: "Matthew doesn't like it!"

Two weeks after Matthew's diagnosis, I was close to despair. The twice daily struggle over the injections was a nightmare that seemed never ending. A telephone call to another mother, whose Down's son needed growth hormone injections, provided a lifeline. She explained how she held her son on her lap, with his legs imprisoned by her legs, so her hands were free to give the injection. I tried this technique and it worked.

The following Sunday, the boys had their first overnight stay at the respite centre. On hearing about Matthew's diabetes, the staff had asked the diabetes nurse to come and teach them how to give blood tests and injections. Their willingness to learn these skills at short notice and take the boys from January as planned, made all the difference to me. The relief of a twenty four hour break from the stresses of Matthew's diabetes was enormous and I firmly believe that these two nights a month of respite (later increased to three nights) saved my family from collapse at this time.

Soon after his first night of respite, Matthew went into what is known as "the honeymoon period". Diabetes develops when most of the insulin producing cells have been destroyed and the remainder are inflamed. After the person starts injecting insulin, the remaining cells sometimes recover and start producing insulin again for a few weeks or months, until they also die. During the second half of January it became clear that his body was producing insulin once more. By the end of January, Matthew needed just one injection a day and by the end of February we were able to suspend injections completely, controlling his blood sugar levels by diet alone.

When Matthew was first diagnosed, one of my reactions had been regret that I had failed to appreciate the freedom we had enjoyed pre-diabetes until it was taken away. Now that part of this freedom had been restored, even for a short while, I was determined to enjoy it and be thankful while it lasted. At the back of my mind there was a faint hope that this might be more than a temporary recovery. Just before Matthew's body started producing insulin again, he had received prayer at church and the elders had subsequently come round to the house to pray for him. Although I knew miraculous healings were rare, I had come across some cases and knew someone personally who had been instantly healed after eight years in a wheelchair as a result of prayer.

Three months later, my hopes were dashed, as Matthew's rising blood sugar levels showed me that I needed to resume injections. For the next nine months, however, he only needed one tiny dose of insulin a day and it was not until three years after diagnosis that his body finally ceased to produce insulin. Such a long "honeymoon period" is extremely unusual and the three month break from insulin injections gave me valuable breathing space as I came to terms with his condition.

On the night I resumed giving injections Daniel was the one showing the most distress. As I injected Matthew, Daniel began sobbing, causing Matthew to go and comfort him. Their concern for each other was the one good thing about that evening. Soon afterwards, the diabetes nurse gave me an automatic injector. The syringe is placed inside this device so that the needle is covered and when a button is pressed, the needle goes quickly into the skin. Matthew soon learnt to press the button himself and the feeling of being in control made him much more co-operative. This in turn made Daniel less distressed at witnessing the injections, although he still liked to give Matthew a cuddle afterwards. When Matthew later moved on to an insulin pen, a similar device was fitted to the pen so that he could press a button to release the needle.

Matthew's diabetes continued to be well controlled until the age of twelve when the hormonal changes of puberty upset his blood sugar levels. At least I could be thankful he wasn't a girl, as the fluctuating levels of female hormones during each month would have made things even more difficult. Reluctantly, we switched to four injections a day, one of long acting insulin each morning and an injection of short acting insulin before each meal. Since then, his blood sugar levels have been among the best of all the children at the diabetes clinic. He can now have a nearly normal diet since I just give him extra insulin if he wants to eat something sweet. Nevertheless, the diabetes has encouraged the whole family to eat more healthily, helping to keep the boys slim, unlike many children with Down's Syndrome.

My mathematical mind has been a huge asset in managing Matthew's diabetes. For each meal, I need to work out roughly how much carbohydrate he will be eating and then calculate the appropriate insulin dose. It is also necessary to look at the pattern of blood sugar levels and use these to decide whether the amount of insulin or the quantity of food needs to be changed. The hardest part is writing instructions to the people caring for Matthew at school and at the respite centre. It is all so complicated that I receive frequent telephone calls asking for advice. As a small child, I once dreamed of becoming a nurse, little realising that I would one day be the personal diabetes nurse for my son.

Over the years Matthew has taken increasing responsibility for his diabetes care and can now do injections all by himself, although I need to check the amount of the dose. He can also do his own blood tests and has some idea of what the results mean. Matthew is very good at recognising the symptoms when his blood sugar dips too low and will always tell me, so that I can give him a sweet drink to bring it up again.

At a special weekend for families of children with diabetes, Matthew proved quite an inspiration to some of the other children when they saw how cheerfully he coped with his double disability. His complete freedom from self pity is certainly an example for me. While he continues to have behaviour problems in other areas, as far as diabetes is concerned he is an absolute star and I am so proud of him.

Chapter 22

Life Goes On

As I was coming to terms with Matthew's diabetes, my boss Brian was facing his own health crisis. During 1999 his cancer became more advanced and he realised the time had come to sell his business. For a while, the only prospective purchasers were firms based some distance away and I was warned that I would soon be made redundant. Although this was a blow, it seemed a small thing compared with Brian's troubles and I could at least be thankful for the four years work I had enjoyed. I did not expect it to be easy to find another job with such flexible hours, especially when I had not used a computer for ten years.

A few months later, however, a new prospective buyer came forward. Not only was this firm based just around the corner from my old office, but the two directors were ex-colleagues from my previous job. They were more than happy to employ me, with my specialist knowledge of the pension schemes they were acquiring and were willing to give me the hours I wanted.

My new actuarial boss, Phil, was in many ways the complete opposite of Brian, easy going and good with people. Our contrasting strengths made us a good team. While Phil went to meetings with the clients, I stayed in the office doing the calculations, an arrangement that suited us both. Phil's only complaint was that it was very boring checking my work, as I made so few mistakes!

Computers had certainly changed a good deal since 1990. It took me a while to get used to this strange new device called a mouse (my boys both learnt to use one long before I did) and the internet was a total mystery. Still, I soon mastered Excel which proved useful for taking some of the drudgery out of calculations, without spoiling the enjoyment.

Once again, I had been given the perfect job for me, without even searching for one.

The boys were growing up fast and were becoming easier to manage within the home. Daniel has become particularly good at amusing himself, playing with his toy animals or his playstation, listening to his CDs, writing stories or watching videos and DVDs. Matthew also enjoys the playstation, as well as doing jigsaws, drawing or playing with playdoh or lego, but he generally prefers adult company to playing on his own. We play many board games together and Matthew is always keen to help with the housework. It can be difficult for me to let him help, as I have my own particular way of doing things. Sometimes I will let him do a task and then secretly do it again later. By contrast, Daniel has generally been reluctant to do household tasks and it has been hard for me to insist when I would much rather do them myself.

Although things became easier at home, outings continued to be difficult. The boys still enjoy the activities they did when they were younger, like going to playgrounds and farms, but now they are much bigger than most of the children at these places, leading to concerns that they might hurt one of them. People have also become much less tolerant of their behaviour as they have grown older. Since they both entered their teens, the agency providing childcare during school holidays has insisted on providing two carers, saying that they are too much for one person to manage.

In recent years, I have tried to find activities that are more age appropriate for the boys. The discovery of a riding school nearby which welcomes special needs proved a great find. Both the boys love riding and Matthew even enjoys mucking out. He has spent several days working at the stables and is really keen to get a job with horses when he grows up. Interestingly, his birth mother was a very keen horsewoman who worked in a riding school before having children, so it would be lovely if he could follow in her footsteps.

Daniel is particularly keen on drama and both boys have had the opportunity to work with a drama group affiliated to

Chicken Shed, which has a mixture of mainstream young people and those with special needs. They also love bowling and I was particularly pleased when they beat several mainstream children at bowling on an outing with the local diabetes support group.

Holidays have become more difficult over the last few years since my mother became too frail to accompany us. On three occasions, I have managed to persuade a friend and her children to come on holiday with us and the friendship has actually survived the experience! It was still hard work, but considerably less stressful than the holidays I have attempted taking the boys on my own, which left me exhausted and badly in need of a holiday.

As the boys have grown older, there have been far more complaints about their behaviour on holidays. Sadly, our worst experiences have been at holiday centres run by Christians. In 2001 we were forced to leave one Christian holiday centre where we had stayed for several years. (This centre has since closed due to declining numbers). Three years later, after two successful holidays at an ordinary hotel, we tried another Christian centre, where we stayed for three years running until we were asked not to return, due to Daniel becoming aggressive when some younger children kept on teasing him. Daniel was also sent home early from a Christian camp for teenagers with special needs because the helpers were unable to cope with his behaviour. They claimed that they needed three people to restrain him to stop him running off, even though I pointed out that I could manage both him and his brother on my own.

I should add that we have also had several good holidays at Christian centres, especially when the boys were younger. Two of our best holidays were provided by Catholic charities. In 2002 we were given a wonderful holiday at Lourdes in France by the Catholic charity HCPT (Handicapped Children's Pilgrimage Trust). Not only did the boys go free, but they each had their own helper, making it a real break for me. More recently, another Catholic charity, S.J.H.C.T (St

John's Handicapped Children's Trust), took the boys on holiday, this time without me and they had a wonderful time.

When Daniel entered his teens, there was the need to consider his sex education. I had already discussed the basic facts, like the differences between boys and girls and where babies came from, at an earlier age. This had led to an awkward situation when a friend visited with her baby and Daniel asked to see the place where the baby had come out. I knew that further information could lead to even more embarrassing moments but it was important for him to know the facts of life, especially as knowledge of appropriate and unacceptable behaviour would help protect him from abuse.

Since Daniel was so good at reading, I was able to buy him a book on growing up and go over some of the topics with him. As a virgin mother, however, I felt a little out of my depth in explaining the facts of life to a teenage boy and was glad when the school decided to do a series of lessons on the subject. Like most teenage boys, Daniel found the subject fascinating and on a few occasions would go up to people saying: "Are you married?"

If they answered in the affirmative, he would then say: "Do you have sex?"

I soon learnt to tell him to stop when he asked the first question. Perhaps Daniel should get a job as a social worker assessing people for adoption. He would then not only be allowed to ask all kinds of intimate questions about their sex lives but also get paid for doing it.

The increasing gap between the boys and their mainstream peers as they grew older was resulting in our family becoming isolated from "normal" families. The children around the same age as mine had left them behind long ago and no longer wanted to visit us. For a time, I tried making friends with families whose children were younger. In some cases this worked well, until these children also outgrew mine, but the size of my boys, together with their boisterous behaviour, meant that many younger children were frightened of them.

At least the boys still had each other, as well as their friends at school who would not outgrow them, but many lived some distance away making it harder to socialise outside school. Being a single parent added to my isolation, as most of the mothers I knew were married and would only visit while their husbands were at work, rather than the weekends, which was always my loneliest time.

Meanwhile, the boys were still attending groups at the church which provided a rota of special helpers for Matthew. This enabled him to attend a group with children of his own age, although he tended to relate mainly to his helper rather than integrating with the other children. Daniel moved at the age of twelve into the youth group but the topics discussed in this group were way over his head, leading to boredom, which in turn could lead to silly behaviour.

Most of the other children had grown up with Daniel and accepted him, although he badly upset the new minister's daughter soon after her arrival by an over enthusiastic hug. Although he was tolerated, I was aware that there was no real friendship. In previous years I had sometimes invited church children to the boys' parties, but they were never invited back, nor did these children want to visit us any more.

By the spring of 2003, I was aware that whilst the church had done its best for my boys, the leaders were feeling increasingly out of their depth. The isolation of being the only parent in the church with children in a special school was also a growing burden. Then an invitation arrived through Daniel's school for the boys to attend an Easter holiday club at another Baptist church a few miles away.

To me, this invitation was amazing. For years, I had been unable to send the boys to the holiday club run by a local church, as a shortage of volunteers meant that they would only accept children with special needs if the parents provided each child with a helper. Since there were two of them and only one of me, this was impossible. Now a church was actually going out of its way to welcome disabled children by sending the invitations to a special school and even providing the helper themselves.

After the Easter holiday club, I learnt that the church had a regular group for children with special needs. One of the leaders was a teacher at Daniel's school and two others were parents of children with special needs. There were three boys who regularly attended the group, all of whom had some form of autism. By now I had put down roots in the church I had been attending for the last nine years and was reluctant to leave my friends. That summer, however, after the boys had enjoyed another holiday club at the new church, I decided that for their sakes I must make the move.

The first Sunday we attended the new church, the assistant minister, who had not realised we would be there, decided to preach a sermon in which he mentioned my boys. By then, I had gone out with the boys to help settle them in to their new group, but I later borrowed a tape and heard the following message:

"All the stuff that the world values – power, position and wealth – does not matter a jot in the kingdom of God. We come in through God's grace and mercy. To represent God's kingdom on earth we have to see the world from God's perspective. The people that Jesus valued and sought out were prostitutes and tax collectors – the most despised people of his day.

All the people in society that we currently reject and marginalize, the vulnerable and the weak, are the very people that God wants to lift up. They are the people that God would love to have in his church and we struggle with it. We need to be honest with this and say to God: "We submit to your authority and kingship and we want to do things your way and not our way."

More and more, I feel that the special needs children and adults are the prophets within our church. They are the people we need to listen to, who are speaking God's truth into the church.

I'll just end with this story about one of the special needs children at holiday club – Daniel . I don't think I'll ever forget this.

At the Easter holiday club we were warned that Daniel gets very emotional and tearful at the crucifixion scene. We acted out the crucifixion and I played Jesus. Sure enough, Daniel burst into tears and was very affected by what was going on. I came down from the cross and lay on the floor, covered in a tent to symbolise being in a tomb. All the children went quiet while I was under this cloth for a period representing three days. Then suddenly someone whipped off the cloth and Daniel ran towards me and hugged me. He said (and I'll never forget this) "Jesus, I've really missed you." That is why Jesus said "I tell you the truth, anyone who will not receive the kingdom of God like a little child will never enter it.""

As the preacher finished his message, I could hear his voice breaking with emotion and I knew that this was the right place for my family.

Chapter 23

"Do you have Asperger Syndrome?"

One evening, in the spring of 2005, I was chatting on the telephone with another mother, Michelle, whose son was in the special needs group at church. In the middle of our conversation, she suddenly said: "Can I ask you a personal question?"

"Yes," I replied, wondering what was coming.

"Do you have Asperger Syndrome?"

Living as I did in the world of special needs, with two sons in special schools, I was well acquainted with all kinds of syndromes. My first introduction to Asperger Syndrome had been through an article in my adopters' magazine in 1996. As I read through the list of characteristics of Asperger Syndrome – social difficulties, taking what people say literally, fears, obsessive interests, need for routine and clumsiness - I immediately recognised myself as a child.

Whilst I had found it helpful to have an explanation for my childhood peculiarities, the knowledge that I had changed so much since then made me think that I must have had only a very mild form of the condition, which I had since outgrown. It certainly did not seem relevant to my life now. In any case, Matthew's subsequent diagnosis with a much more obvious and life threatening condition had pushed my possible Asperger Syndrome to the back of my mind.

Lately, however, I had become increasingly aware that the problems of my childhood had not gone away completely. Some recent social blunders, one of which had nearly lost me my closest friend, had left me deeply discouraged. Why, after thirty years of trying so hard to learn the social rules, during which I had been willing to accept all kinds of criticism and learn from my mistakes, was I still getting things wrong? Why did I have to work so hard at my friendships when other people seemed to attract friends without trying? Why did I, as a supposedly mature woman in my late forties, still have such trouble controlling my tongue and my emotions in public?

In my twenties I had assumed, as the psychiatrists and various counsellors had done, that all my problems stemmed from my upbringing, but in recent years I had begun to doubt this. Whilst the tensions in my childhood home had no doubt contributed to my emotional difficulties, I knew several people who had experienced much more traumatic childhoods with less apparent damage and fewer social problems.

On hearing Michelle's question, I made up my mind. I would get a proper assessment and find out for certain whether I did have a genuine problem, or was just selfish, immature and rude, as so many people had suggested over the years.

For my mother's sake, I was also anxious to know the truth. I knew she had often blamed herself and been blamed by others, for the problems we children had experienced. If she knew that at least one of her children had a genuine disability, it would be easier for her to forgive herself. She was now in her late seventies and had already suffered two minor heart attacks so I felt an urgency to discover the truth while she was still alive.

I did not expect it to be easy to obtain a diagnosis at my age. Even if I had the condition, thirty years of striving to be normal had surely diminished the Asperger characteristics to such an extent that it would be very hard to spot them. Michelle assured me, however, that it was obvious to her that I had Asperger Syndrome. Despite this, she warned me against obtaining a formal diagnosis, as it was too late for me to receive any help for the condition and she feared that the Asperger label might make people see me just as someone with Aspergers, rather than looking at me as an ordinary person.

I assured Michelle that I already had a label, as the mother of two children with Down's Syndrome. This was far more obvious than any other label and it would make a change to have a different one. The day that Matthew had been diagnosed with diabetes, I had heard a nurse say to the doctor coming on duty:

"This is Matthew, who is diabetic."

Amid all the trauma of the new diagnosis, there was almost a sense of relief that for once he was not being viewed primarily as a child with Down's Syndrome.

One concern I did have was that a diagnosis of Aspergers might count against me when applying for medical insurance or even car insurance. There was also the danger that social workers might decide it made me an unfit mother, although I did not think that anyone would actually remove two teenage boys who had been with me since babyhood and had been legally adopted.

Since I knew it was unlikely that I would qualify for an assessment under the National Health Service, I found details of a private assessment centre and wrote to them. In my letter, I described my life history and the reasons why I thought I had Asperger Syndrome. Part of me expected the psychologist to write back, saying:

"Don't be ridiculous. Whoever heard of someone with Asperger Syndrome adopting two Down's boys? Of course you haven't got it."

Instead, however, I received a telephone call from the centre saying that they thought I might have the condition and offering me an assessment in about six weeks time.

In reply to my concerns about insurance, the psychologist Dr Davis said that there would be no need to disclose my diagnosis, as it was a social disorder rather than a medical condition. The assessment itself was expensive, but I felt it was a small price to pay for an end to uncertainty.

While waiting for my appointment I read Dr Tony Attwood's book *Asperger's Syndrome: A Guide for Parents and Professionals* (Jessica Kingsley Publishers). Some of the descriptions of the loneliness, bullying and isolation experienced by children and teenagers with the syndrome brought my childhood memories flooding back with painful intensity. By the time I had finished, I knew I had the condition, but would the psychologist agree, who would only have the opportunity to see me now as a relatively normal adult?

The day of my assessment, like so many other important days in my life (including my birth), fell on a Thursday. Knowing that my own opinion of myself was bound to be biased, I brought with me some appraisals from my second employer, which gave a good summary of my strengths and weaknesses. For two hours, Dr Davis asked me questions about my life and my family. After talking until I was hoarse, I sat back to await the verdict.

"You definitely have Asperger Syndrome," she told me. "There is no doubt about it."

From the things I had told her, she was also convinced that Asperger Syndrome ran in my family, down the male line, although I had the dubious distinction of being the only female in my family with the condition.

My overwhelming reaction was relief. I had not been imagining things, or making excuses for bad behaviour. Instead, I had a genuine disability. When I had difficulty in relating to others it was not because I was more selfish than the average person, nor was I uninterested in people. I desperately wanted to relate to people and get close to them but was hampered by my inability to understand their unspoken language.

Dr Davis explained that the latest research indicated that Asperger Syndrome is due to lack of development of the parts of the brain responsible for social awareness and flexibility. Suddenly I understood why I tended to get upset when something unexpected happened. It was hard for my brain to work out quickly how to respond to the unforeseen event, so the natural reaction was to panic. This was why I needed to order my life and have set routines, to enable me to cope.

A great load of guilt was shed as it was explained that I could not help my social blunders, any more than someone living in an alien culture who has not been told the rules. My lack of awareness when I upset people, unless they made it very obvious, was not due to callousness or unconcern for other people's feelings, but resulted from my inability to read their body language, a kind of "social dyslexia".

Amid the relief, there was one major concern: could my social difficulties have harmed my children in any way? They had certainly done wonders for me, helping to modify many of my Asperger traits, as well as giving me their unconditional love and acceptance, but had I been good for them? As we discussed it, Dr Davis expressed the opinion that my Aspergers would have made me an unsuitable parent for a child who was emotionally damaged, like most children available for adoption, but by some instinct I had chosen the children who were right for me. Thinking it through later, I could see the reasons why we made such a good team.

Like me, my children say exactly what they think, so we understand each other. Whereas other children might show subtle signs of distress that I might fail to notice, mine express their needs and hurts so loudly that they cannot be ignored. Having made so many social gaffes myself, there is little that my children can do to embarrass me (although they try very hard) and my indifference to peer pressure enables me to enjoy having children who are different from the norm. My preference for fixed routines gives them structure and stability which is important for children with learning disabilities and is particularly helpful in managing Matthew's diabetes.

Having said that, I am sure there have been times when my Asperger's has resulted in a failure to understand my children's needs, or to be the calm, mature role model they required. Still, they seem to have survived relatively unscathed and I know they are better off with me than with no-one to love them. I daresay there are many people who could have made a better job of bringing up my boys, but where were they when my children needed a home?

Chapter 24

Coming Out

My family were the first people to whom I revealed my diagnosis. They were already aware that I had requested an assessment so it was not a complete surprise. For my sister, it merely confirmed what she had already thought: that Asperger Syndrome ran in our family, although we both agreed that she had escaped. My mother seemed to greet the diagnosis with a mixture of scepticism and relief but my brother had a more negative response. Simon warned me against telling people, saying that it would stop them from taking me seriously and they would use it as an excuse to patronise me.

I could not agree with this opinion. In my experience, those who are open about their weaknesses instead of hiding them generally find that people like and respect them more for their honesty and will often open up to them in their turn, leading to deeper friendship. There will always be some people who will use such knowledge against you, but they are not the ones whose respect matters to me. In any case, openness is part of my nature. Like Darcy, I would say:

"Disguise of every sort is my abhorrence." (*Pride and Prejudice*, chapter 34)

In addition, I identified strongly with the reaction of the apostle Paul to his disability, when he said:

"Three times I pleaded with the Lord to take it away from me. But he said to me, "My grace is sufficient for you, for my power is made perfect in weakness." Therefore, I will boast all the more gladly about my weaknesses, so that Christ's power may rest on me." (2 Corinthians 12 v 8, 9)

When considering whether to "come out" I had the example of two transsexual friends with whom I had discussed the relative merits of secrecy and disclosure. One of them, Natalie, had chosen to be open with her church about her past life with a male body and had received an overwhelmingly positive response. This was largely due to the minister who had been prepared to research her condition (gender dysphoria), examine what the Bible had to say with an open mind and explain it to the church members. The advantages of openness included the opportunity to educate people and help eliminate prejudice, as well as the chance to be yourself without worrying about accidentally giving the game away. Natalie did say, however, that she felt people looked at her first as a transsexual rather than as Natalie and had subsequently chosen to keep quiet about her past at her new job, in the hope that she could be treated just as an ordinary woman, a privilege most of us take for granted.

One interesting parallel between my condition and that of my transsexual friends was that people with Asperger Syndrome have been described as having an extreme male brain. There is a theory that it is caused by excess testosterone in the womb. In the same way, gender dysphoria is believed to be due to the female foetus receiving too much testosterone or, more commonly, the male foetus receiving too little.

When I was younger, I used to think that I had a man's mind, but a woman's desires and emotions. Whilst I believe some women with Asperger Syndrome have felt confused over their gender identity, I always identified strongly as female and longed to be more feminine, partly because I found that women who talk and argue like men tend to be shunned by men and women alike. Perhaps one reason I can relate well to transgender people is that we both recognise that all of us have some male and female characteristics. (In fact, the intersex condition, where the body is partly male and partly female, is as common as Down's Syndrome.) Instead of expecting people to conform to gender stereotypes, we can accept people as they are.

For me, coming out was clearly far less risky than for Natalie, but was it necessary? Just as Natalie had reached the stage where she passed quite well as a woman, I could now

145

pass as normal to most people, except when stressed, but the strain of pretending to be like everyone else was getting to be too much. Besides, all my life I had longed for people to understand me instead of judging me by their own rules.

Telling close friends was easy. Kate had suspected for a long time that I had the condition and regarded the confirmation as a cause for celebration. She is the total opposite of me, tending to go along with other people's opinions and wishes for the sake of peace, as well as being acutely sensitive to body language and hating maths. Although this has sometimes led to misunderstandings, we have been able to learn a great deal from each other.

My church was another place where I could be sure of a positive response, with their enlightened attitude to people with disabilities. The Sunday after my diagnosis, we had a visiting speaker from the charity "Through the Roof", which aims to make churches more supportive of people with all kinds of disabilities. The name comes from the story of the four men who brought their paralysed friend to Jesus, but when they could not get through the door, they made a hole in the roof and lowered him down to where Jesus was sitting. I had already been a supporter of this charity for some years and had signed up for the holiday they were planning for families with disabled children.

That Sunday I submitted an article for the church newsletter, explaining about my diagnosis. When it was published the following Sunday, one or two people expressed surprise, others interest and one lady (a fellow mathematician) said that she thought she might also have it. My main hope in writing was that people would understand that I really do want to make friends with them, even if I am unwittingly giving out the opposite message by my body language. On a couple of occasions in church, I have accidentally caught someone's eye and they have smiled at me. Although I knew I should smile back, instead I quickly looked away in embarrassment. In some churches the congregation are asked to say the prayer called the grace to each other, looking round and catching as many people's eyes as possible. During such times I have had to work extra hard to avoid eye contact, usually by looking down at the floor, or making sure I look at people while their backs are turned.

Just a week after diagnosis, armed with some leaflets on Asperger Syndrome written for employers, I came out at work. I explained that I was not asking for special treatment, but wanted people to understand that I might unwittingly upset or annoy someone and would not realise I had done it, because of my difficulties in reading body language. If a problem arose, I asked them to tell me directly, but try to do it gently, realising that I had not meant to cause offence.

This also provided an opportunity to explain why I had been so upset a couple of years earlier when I had come into work to find that two new people had just arrived, a new director and his secretary and the secretary had been awarded my parking space. At the time they had thought me very unreasonable to complain when they were offering to pay my parking fees at the multi-storey car park, not realising how stressful parking is for me at the best of times, with my very poor spatial awareness. By the time of my diagnosis, the departure of another member of staff had solved the parking problem, but the anxiety over the same thing happening again had remained.

Generally, people at work were very understanding and since that time Phil always made a point of warning me in advance about any changes, which was really helpful. The office manager, Janice, subsequently discovered that her own adult son had dyspraxia, which has some features in common with Asperger's, although it is a different condition. I think she found it useful talking to someone who also had experience of an invisible disability.

One Friday, Janice and I were chatting about our plans for the weekend and I mentioned that I was having some friends round for tea that Sunday. Later, as I was about to leave, she said: "Enjoy your tea party tomorrow."

Without thinking, I replied: "It's on Sunday" and left the office. Later, I realised how rude that must have sounded and on Monday I apologised to Janice, explaining that the Asperger obsession with getting the facts right had made me forget that politeness was far more important. Fortunately, she had not been offended but I was glad of the chance to explain.

At first I was unsure whether to share my diagnosis with my sons. Daniel has always shown a keen interest in the syndromes of the children at his school and a few years ago there was a boy in his class with Asperger's (although I believe he had other problems as well). This child was seriously disruptive and was eventually sent to boarding school because his obsession with fire meant that he kept trying to burn his house down. Since then we had become friendly with another Asperger boy who was highly intelligent and better behaved than many "normal" children, but would Daniel still assume that arson was an Asperger trait and fear that I might set fire to our house? Fortunately he seemed quite happy with my news, although at the next visit to the optician he introduced us saying:

"I'm Daniel and I've got Down's Syndrome. This is my brother Matthew who has Down's Syndrome and this is my Mum Fiona who has Asperger Syndrome."

At least it made a change from him telling people my age, but I knew that revealing my condition to Daniel was effectively broadcasting it to the whole world.

When telling the boys' schools about my Asperger's, there was no need to give them information on the condition, since both were special schools with a number of children on the autistic spectrum. I suspect the staff at Daniel's school had already guessed long before they received my letter. At Matthew's school, I broke the news during one of the regular meetings to discuss strategies for dealing with Matthew's behaviour, saying that perhaps my diagnosis provided some explanation for his problems. To my relief, the deputy head, Mrs Rivers, immediately said that she thought Matthew's behaviour was typical of a child with Down's Syndrome. My social worker also reassured me, pointing out that my Asperger's had probably helped me to provide a structured environment for the boys.

It was at one of these meetings at Matthew's school that my inability to remember a face led to an embarrassing blunder. Mrs Rivers said that Matthew's behaviour had improved a good deal since he had moved to that school at the age of ten. At this point, I recalled an incident in the first term, when his class teacher had telephoned me in a panic, because he had flatly refused to get in his taxi.

"That was me," Mrs Rivers said.

I looked at her in astonishment. Surely his first class teacher had been Mrs Jones? It was only after the meeting that I realised that Mrs Jones might have remarried and changed her name. All this time I had been assuming that Mrs Rivers was a new teacher, since I could not remember his first teacher's face.

Recently, the mother of an autistic boy told me that when his brother's voice broke, her son assumed that this was a new person and could not believe it was his brother. My confusion over the teacher having a different name, despite knowing that people do change their names, helped me to understand how bewildered he must have felt.

Shortly after my diagnosis, on a visit to the chiropodist I discovered that her husband, who was a mature student at university, had just been diagnosed with severe dyslexia. The report on his diagnosis stated that he must have worked incredibly hard to have achieved so much despite this disability. My chiropodist said that her husband had shown this report to his tutor, who had previously accused him of laziness, to show him how wrong he had been. I knew exactly how he felt, remembering those who had misjudged me.

One big danger of my new discovery was the temptation to sink back into self-pity and resentment, as the full extent of my difficulties became clear. For this reason I asked my minister and one of the women leaders at the church to come and pray with me about all the hurts I had received and help me to go through the process of forgiving each person who had misunderstood or misjudged me. It was an emotionally exhausting experience, but immensely helpful in letting go of the past and moving on. I also needed to forgive myself for all the people I had hurt, either unwittingly or sometimes on purpose. Throughout my adult life I have tried to apologise to those I know I have offended, but there may be many more of whom I am unaware. All I can do is hope that they are willing to forgive me.

Receiving my diagnosis in middle age has the advantage that I now know enough of the world to realise most people have something that makes their life very difficult. It could be the grinding poverty affecting more than half the people on this planet, or living under an oppressive regime, experiences of abuse or a disability. When I consider the total suffering in this world, I know that even with the loneliness resulting from Asperger's (the pain of which can still be hard to bear at times), I probably have less than my fair share of troubles. In any case, each experience of suffering, whether fear, bereavement, loneliness, childlessness or disability, brings you closer to others who have been through similar problems, which can lead to the deep friendships that I have craved all my life.

Chapter 25

Looking to the Future

A few months after my diagnosis, I was resting at home one Thursday, trying to shake off a persistent virus, when the telephone rang. It was the deputy head teacher at Daniel's school. After making the usual polite enquiry after my health and receiving a longer answer than expected, since in all honesty I could not say I was fine, she got to the point.

"We want your permission to have Daniel tested for autism."

If someone had said that to me a few years earlier, I would have been incredulous and horrified. How could someone as loving and caring as Daniel possibly have autism? His main behaviour problem is his habit of wanting to hug and kiss everyone. If people are ill or upset, Daniel will be the first to go and comfort them. He also has a huge capacity for enjoying life and loves new experiences. Far from being reluctant to communicate, his speech has always been remarkably good for someone with his learning difficulties. Could anyone be less like the image I had in my mind of the withdrawn, deeply unhappy autistic child, who communicated only through screams?

Since my own diagnosis, however, I had noticed some traits in Daniel that suggested he might have some mild form of autism, possibly Asperger Syndrome. His hypersensitivity to noise, even when not wearing his hearing aid, has increased over the last couple of years. He has always been highly emotional, getting excited or upset very easily and overreacting to teasing. Having a brother who delights in winding people up has not helped, since his overreaction merely encourages Matthew to do it all the more. Although Daniel always greets any visitors with enthusiasm, he will frequently leave them to their own devices and go off to his bedroom, even when they are his special friends. He certainly enjoys his own company and talks to himself a great deal, although this latter trait is common in people with Down's Syndrome as well as those with autism.

One thing that has caused particular concern is Daniel's lack of awareness of the effect of his behaviour on others, although it is hard to tell whether this arises from his general learning difficulties or something else. A few months after the incident with the minister's daughter, Daniel tried to go up to her again and give her a hug. Even I could see the fear expressed by her body language, but Daniel either could not see it or chose to ignore it, forcing me to intervene.

When Daniel was fourteen, a psychological assessment had shown a very uneven pattern of skills. Whilst his reading age was nine, his general comprehension was much lower, around the five year old level and his social reasoning skills were lower still. He was said to be at the pre-reasoning stage, so could not understand the consequences of his actions, which was why discipline had so little effect. In some ways the assessment had come as a relief, as it showed that his difficult behaviours were not due to poor parenting, as some had suggested, but arose from his lack of understanding.

The large gap between Daniel's academic ability and social skills, together with his emotional immaturity and lack of common sense, reminded me strongly of myself. With no genetic link between us, he could not have inherited my Asperger's, but could he have copied some of my behaviours? Whilst this may be the case, I suspect that Asperger Syndrome was present in Daniel's birth family. When I first read the description of Daniel's birth father in the social worker's letter about his background, the thought struck me that they could have been talking about my paternal grandfather.

The school had clearly suspected for some time that Daniel had autistic tendencies. In September, they had moved him from his previous group to a class that was mainly for pupils on the autistic spectrum. Whilst somewhat surprised by the decision, I knew that there had been problems with the previous class and Daniel had complained of being bullied. His best friend was in the autistic group, which helped to reconcile me to the change. The improvement in his happiness and behaviour in his new class convinced the school that Daniel had some form of autism, hence their telephone call to me.

After putting the telephone down, I sank into a chair and tried to take in this news. Unlike the diabetes, this was no new condition affecting my family. If Daniel did have some form of autism, then like me, he must have been born with it. I had always declared that I could never cope with an autistic child, yet if the school were right, that was exactly what I had been doing for the past sixteen years. What is more, far from being an ordeal, it had been the best experience of my life. Despite some trying behaviours and the usual grumpiness of adolescence, Daniel was still a very lovable person. An autism label would not change him into some kind of monster, but could be helpful in explaining some of his difficulties and showing people how best to help him.

When the psychologist came round to discuss the assessment, I said that Daniel was unlikely to have classic autism (sometimes called Kanner's Syndrome), but I believed he had Asperger Syndrome. She told me that Daniel was not intelligent enough to have Asperger Syndrome and insisted on doing a test for classic autism, which unsurprisingly gave a negative result. The school and I remained convinced that Daniel had some form of autism, so I requested a reassessment, which was at first refused. After two years it was finally agreed to refer Daniel to another psychologist for a second opinion. At the time of writing (June 2008), this psychologist has just completed her assessment. Her conclusion is that Daniel has complex needs, including several autistic traits, but does not quite fit the profile for autism or Asperger Syndrome. The only thing that she can say with certainty is that he is "not your normal Down's youth".

Whether or not Daniel is on the autistic spectrum, it has become increasingly clear over the last few years that his lack of understanding and immature social skills make him extremely vulnerable. I used to hope that Daniel would attend the local further education college and continue to live at home after leaving school, but his teachers realized long before I did that he would not be able to cope. Since November 2004 I have been trying to find the right specialist residential college, where Daniel can go after leaving school in the summer of 2008 and learn independent living skills, as well as receiving vocational training and enjoying a good social life with his peers, just as I did at university.

Little did I imagine when I started my search for a college, just how difficult it would be to obtain a place for Daniel. To be on the safe side I visited six special needs colleges all over the country and applied to four of them. One by one each college turned him down, citing his immature behaviour and in one case his aggression to another student in response to being teased. When the fourth rejection came through, in November 2007, I was close to despair. By now nearly all the colleges were full for 2008 and many for 2009 as well. Just one thing kept me going: the memory of how hopeless my life had seemed when I was Daniel's age, in August 1975 and how my life had subsequently been transformed over the next few months.

As a last resort, I was advised to try a specialist college in my county, which three years earlier had been rejected both by me and the careers advisor as unsuitable for Daniel. Amazingly, they still had places left and subsequent visits showed that this was indeed the right college. Over the last three years this college has improved and expanded, accepting a broader range of students so that Daniel now has an appropriate peer group. There is a farm at the college, including pigs which are Daniel's great love. (The story of the prodigal son would be lost on Daniel, who would see working with pigs as an incentive to leave home.) The college staff have plenty of experience in managing difficult behaviours and were very understanding when Daniel became distressed at the noise of building works and later at the yelping noises made by a student with Tourette's Syndrome on a visit to the college. Best of all, the college is half an hour's drive from our home, unlike some of the colleges visited which involved four or five hours travelling time each way. When confirmation finally came in April 2008 that Daniel had a place at this college (subject to funding), I was too exhausted with the stress of it all to feel anything other than profound relief.

Daniel is very keen to go away to college and he certainly needs more independence than I can give him. At home, he cannot even play on his own in the garden without complaints from the neighbours about him making inappropriate remarks or throwing things over the fence. He will stay at the college for weekends, just coming home for half term and holidays. I will miss him terribly, but I know now that it is for the best. After his three years at college, the plan is for him to move into some kind of supported housing nearby, where he can use the independence skills acquired at college, but still have regular visits home.

Matthew will definitely miss his brother when he goes to college, but their quarrels have increased since they both reached puberty and a break from each other will probably do them good. It will also give Matthew the chance to enjoy my undivided attention and I will be able to manage more outings with just one son at home. Matthew really wants to go to a college where he can work with horses and we have already begun visiting suitable specialist colleges.

One of the concerns I have for the boys is that they will have the opportunity to grow in their faith once they have left home. At present they have a special group geared to their needs, where they can go during the sermon, but very few churches offer such a facility even for disabled children, much less for adults. The Christian charity Prospects supports Bible study groups for adults with learning disabilities as well as providing Christian residential homes, but the demand far outstrips the supply. Both boys have a faith of their own and are particularly keen on praying for those who are ill. Daniel was baptised at his own request when he was seventeen and was so excited that he was dancing for joy in the pool used for the baptism. Matthew has also asked to be baptised, although I feel he needs to wait until he is a little older and understands that there is more to it than just being the centre of attention for one day.

Plans for my own future are rather less clear. One unexpected change in the autumn of 2006 was my redundancy. A reduction in the amount of work available meant that my firm could no longer offer me three days work a week, although for a few months they gave me a temporary contract for a reduced number of hours. Although a shock at first, this has proved a blessing in disguise, providing a much needed rest, as well as time to plan Daniel's future and now to write this book. Having celebrated my fiftieth birthday the month before my job ended, I no longer have the energy needed to be a full time carer and go out to work even part time, especially now that the boys go to bed later and I have lost my free evenings. The time has now come to concentrate on my caring role, which fortunately I can afford to do.

As for the longer term, much will depend on the amount of support my sons will continue to need from me after they have officially left home, as well as on my future health. I have started doing some maths tutoring for the children of friends and hope to do more once Matthew is at college. I would also love to do some voluntary work, supporting families affected by disability. On a recent holiday with the charity "Through the Roof", which was primarily for families with autistic children, I found that my own experience of Asperger Syndrome, together with caring for children with special needs, enabled me to relate to the other parents and gave me insight into their children's fears and behaviour. Most of my own fears, which seem so odd to "normal" people, are common in those affected by autism, yet many autistic people are unable to voice their anxieties and can only show them by their behaviour. Those of us who share these traits but are able to communicate can provide a bridge of understanding between the autistic and the "normal" worlds.

Whatever the future holds, one thing is certain: although my sons and I may not all live together under the same roof for much longer, we will always be a family, bound together by something closer than a blood tie. Despite all the difficulties, knowing them has enriched my life beyond description. Never would I have guessed, as a teenager living in a fantasy world, that my life would one day be far more interesting and fulfilling than any of these fantasies, thanks to my two special sons and above all to God "who is able to do immeasurably more than all we ask or imagine, according to his power that is at work within us" (Ephesians 3. 20).

Appendix 1 - What is Asperger Syndrome?

(This is an abridged version of the description of Asperger Syndrome on the website www.autism.org.uk/asperger, reproduced with kind permission of The National Autistic Society 2008.)

As soon as we meet a person we make judgements about them. From their facial expression, tone of voice and body language we can usually tell whether they are happy, angry or sad and respond accordingly.

People with Asperger syndrome can find it harder to read the signals that most of us take for granted. This means they find it more difficult to communicate and interact with others which can lead to high levels of anxiety and confusion.

Asperger syndrome is a form of autism, which is a lifelong disability that affects how a person makes sense of the world, processes information and relates to other people. Autism is often described as a 'spectrum disorder' because the condition affects people in many different ways and to varying degrees.

Asperger syndrome is mostly a 'hidden disability'. This means that you can't tell that someone has the condition from their outward appearance. People with the condition have difficulties in three main areas. They are:

- social communication
- social interaction
- social imagination.

They are often referred to as 'the triad of impairments' and are explained in more detail below.

While there are similarities with autism, people with

159

Asperger syndrome have fewer problems with speaking and are often of average, or above average, intelligence. They do not usually have the accompanying learning disabilities associated with autism, but they may have specific learning difficulties. These may include dyslexia and dyspraxia or other conditions such as attention deficit hyperactivity disorder (ADHD) and epilepsy.

With the right support and encouragement, people with Asperger syndrome can lead full and independent lives.

What are the characteristics of Asperger syndrome?

The characteristics of Asperger syndrome vary from one person to another but are generally divided into three main groups.

Difficulty with social communication

"If you have Asperger syndrome, understanding conversation is like trying to understand a foreign language."

People with Asperger syndrome sometimes find it difficult to express themselves emotionally and socially. For example, they may:

- have difficulty understanding gestures, facial expressions or tone of voice
- have difficulty knowing when to start or end a conversation and choosing topics to talk about
- use complex words and phrases but may not fully understand what they mean
- be very literal in what they say and can have difficulty understanding jokes, metaphor and sarcasm. For example, a person with Asperger syndrome may be confused by the phrase 'That's cool' when people use it

to say something is good.

In order to help a person with Asperger syndrome understand you, keep your sentences short - be clear and concise.

Difficulty with social interaction

"I have difficulty picking up social cues, and difficulty in knowing what to do when I get things wrong."

Many people with Asperger syndrome want to be sociable but have difficulty with initiating and sustaining social relationships, which can make them very anxious. People with the condition may:

- struggle to make and maintain friendships
- not understand the unwritten 'social rules' that most of us pick up without thinking. For example, they may stand too close to another person, or start an inappropriate topic of conversation
- find other people unpredictable and confusing
- become withdrawn and seem uninterested in other people, appearing almost aloof
- behave in what may seem an inappropriate manner.

Difficulty with social imagination

"We have trouble working out what other people know. We have more difficulty guessing what other people are thinking."

People with Asperger syndrome can be imaginative in the conventional use of the word. For example, many are accomplished writers, artists and musicians. But people with Asperger syndrome can have difficulty with social imagination. This can include:

- imagining alternative outcomes to situations and finding it hard to predict what will happen next
- understanding or interpreting other peoples thoughts, feelings or actions. The subtle messages that are put across by facial expression and body language are often missed
- having a limited range of imaginative activities, which can be pursued rigidly and repetitively eg lining up toys or collecting and organising things related to his or her interest.

Some children with Asperger syndrome may find it difficult to play 'let's pretend' games or prefer subjects rooted in logic and systems, such as mathematics.

Other related characteristics

Love of routines

"If I get anxious I get in a tizz. I have a timetable; it helps me to see what I have to do next, otherwise I get confused."

To try and make the world less confusing, people with Asperger syndrome may have rules and rituals (ways of doing things) which they insist upon. Young children, for example, may insist on always walking the same way to school. In class, they may get upset if there is a sudden change to the timetable. People with Asperger syndrome often prefer to order their day to a set pattern. For example, if they work set hours, an unexpected delay to their journey to or from work can make them anxious or upset.

Special interests

"I remember Samuel reciting the distances of all the planets from the sun to a baffled classmate in the playground when he was five. Since then he has had many obsessions, which he loves to talk about at length!"

People with Asperger syndrome may develop an intense, sometimes obsessive, interest in a hobby or collecting. Sometimes these interests are lifelong; in other cases, one interest is replaced by an unconnected interest. For example, a person with Asperger syndrome may focus on learning all there is to know about trains or computers. Some are exceptionally knowledgeable in their chosen field of interest. With encouragement, interests and skills can be developed so that people with Asperger syndrome can study or work in their favourite subjects.

Sensory difficulties

"Robert only has problems with touch when he doesn't know what's coming - like jostling in queues and people accidentally brushing into him. Light touch seems to be worse for him than a firm touch."

People with Asperger syndrome may have sensory difficulties. These can occur in one or all of the senses (sight, sound, smell, touch, or taste). The degree of difficulty varies from one individual to another. Most commonly, an individual's senses are either intensified (over-sensitive) or underdeveloped (under-sensitive). For example, bright lights, loud noises, overpowering smells, particular food textures and the feeling of certain materials can be a cause of anxiety and pain for people with Asperger syndrome.

People with sensory sensitivity may also find it harder to use their body awareness system. This system tells us where our bodies are, so for those with reduced body awareness, it can be harder to navigate rooms avoiding obstructions, stand at an appropriate distance from other people and carry out 'fine motor' tasks such as tying shoelaces. Some people with Asperger syndrome may rock or spin to help with balance and posture or to help them deal with stress.

Who is affected by Asperger syndrome?

There are over half a million people in the UK with an autism spectrum disorder - that's around 1 in 100. People with Asperger syndrome come from all nationalities, cultures, social backgrounds and religions. However, the condition appears to be more common in males than females; the reason for this is unknown.

What causes Asperger syndrome?

The exact cause of Asperger syndrome is still being investigated. However, research suggests that a combination of factors - genetic and environmental - may account for changes in brain development.

Asperger syndrome is not caused by a person's upbringing, their social circumstances and is not the fault of the individual with the condition.

Is there a cure?

There is currently no cure and no specific treatment for Asperger syndrome. Children with Asperger syndrome become adults with Asperger syndrome. However, as our understanding of the condition improves and services continue to develop, people with Asperger syndrome have more opportunity than ever of reaching their full potential.

There are many approaches, therapies and interventions, which can improve an individual's quality of life. These may include communication-based interventions, behavioural therapy and dietary changes. Information about many of these can be found on The National Autistic Society's website at: www.autism.org.uk/approaches

What is a diagnosis?

Because Asperger syndrome varies widely from person to person, making a diagnosis can be difficult. It is often diagnosed later in children than autism and sometimes difficulties may not be recognised and diagnosed until adulthood. The typical route for getting a diagnosis is to visit a GP. He or she can refer an individual to other health professionals who can make a formal diagnosis. Most frequently they will be psychiatrists or clinical psychologists and, in the case of children, paediatricians.

Some people see a formal diagnosis as an unhelpful label; however, for many a diagnosis:

- helps the individual, families, friends, partners, carers, professionals and colleagues to better understand and manage their needs and behaviour
- is the key needed to open the door to specialised support, eg supported living or finding suitable employment.

There are diagnostic differences between conditions on the autism spectrum. Sometimes people may receive a diagnosis of autism or autistic spectrum disorder (ASD), high-functioning autism (HFA) or atypical autism instead of Asperger syndrome. Alternatively, they may be given a diagnosis of pervasive developmental disorder - not otherwise

165

specified (PDD-NOS) or semantic pragmatic disorder. However, people who have been given these diagnoses will have similar difficulties and similar support needs to those who have Asperger syndrome.

Appendix 2 Useful Organisations

The National Autistic Society (NAS)
(Supports those with autism and Asperger Syndrome and their families)
393 City Road
London
EC1V 1NG
Tel: 020 7833 2299
Website: www.autism.org.uk
Helpline: 0845 070 4004 (open 10am-4pm, Monday-Friday)
Email: autismhelpline@nas.org.uk

Down's Syndrome Association
(Supports people with Down's Syndrome and their families)
Langdon Down Centre
2a Langdon Park
Teddington
Middlesex
TW11 9PS
Tel: 0845 230 0372
Email: info@downs-syndrome.org.uk
Website: www.downs-syndrome.org.uk

Adoption UK
(Supports adoptive families before, during and after adoption)
46 The Green
South Bar Street
Banbury
Oxfordshire
OX16 9AB
Tel: 01295 752240
Email:admin@adoptionUK.org.uk
Helpline (England and Wales): 0844 848 7900

Diabetes UK
(Supports those with diabetes and their families)

10 Parkway
London
NW1 7AA
Tel: 020 7424 1000
Email: info@diabetes.org.uk
Website: www.diabetes.org.uk
Helpline: 0845 120 2960 (open 9am-5pm Monday –Friday)

UK Paruresis Trust (UKPT)
(Helps people who find it difficult or impossible to urinate in a public or social situation.)
PO Box 182
Kendal
Cumbria LA9 9AE
Email: support@ukpt.org.uk
Website: www.ukpt.org.uk

Through The Roof
(Supports people with disabilities and their families, as well as helping the church to value those with disabilities as equal members of God's family.)
PO Box 353
Epsom
Surrey KT18 5WS
Tel: 01372 749955
Email: info@throughthe roof.org
Website:www.throughtheroof.org

Prospects
(A Christian charity providing homes and supporting Bible study groups for people with learning disabilities)
69 Honey End Lane
Reading
Berkshire RG30 4EL
Tel: 0118 950 8781
Website: www.prospects.org.uk

Hamlin Fistula UK
(This charity, mentioned in chapter 3, supports a wonderful hospital in Ethiopia, transforming the lives of women and girls who suffer incontinence, desperate poverty and social ostracism as a result of childbirth injury.)
Bradfield House
Popes Lane
Oldbury
West Midlands B69 4PA
Tel: 0121 544 7772
Website: www.hamlinfistulauk.org

Alpha International
Alpha International
Holy Trinity Brompton
Brompton Road
London
SW7 1JA
Website: alpha.org

The Alpha courses, which are run throughout the UK and overseas, are designed for those who do not normally attend church but have questions about the Christian faith and these courses are open to all. Each session usually comprises a meal or refreshments, followed by a talk and then discussion in small groups. Many people have found these courses helpful in examining the evidence for and against the Christian faith and in learning how they can experience the power of the Holy Spirit (see chapter 6, although this course was not available when I was searching for the truth).